PLOUGHSHARES

Spring 1998 · Vol. 24,

GUEST EDITORS
Stuart Dybek &
Jane Hirshfield

EDITOR
Don Lee

POETRY EDITOR
David Daniel

ASSOCIATE EDITOR
Susan Conley

ASSISTANT FICTION EDITOR
Maryanne O'Hara

FOUNDING EDITOR
DeWitt Henry

FOUNDING PUBLISHER
Peter O'Malley

ADVISORY EDITORS

Russell Banks
Ann Beattie
Anne Bernays
Frank Bidart
Robert Boswell
Rosellen Brown
James Carroll
Madeline DeFrees
Rita Dove
Andre Dubus
Carolyn Forché
Richard Ford
George Garrett
Lorrie Goldensohn
Mary Gordon
David Gullette
Marilyn Hacker
Donald Hall
Paul Hannigan
Stratis Haviaras

DeWitt Henry
Fanny Howe
Marie Howe
Justin Kaplan
Bill Knott
Yusef Komunyakaa
Maxine Kumin
Philip Levine
Thomas Lux
Gail Mazur
James Alan McPherson
Leonard Michaels
Sue Miller
Jay Neugeboren
Howard Norman
Tim O'Brien
Joyce Peseroff
Jayne Anne Phillips
Robert Pinsky
James Randall

Alberto Alvaro Ríos
Lloyd Schwartz
Jane Shore
Charles Simic
Gary Soto
Maura Stanton
Gerald Stern
Mark Strand
Christopher Tilghman
Richard Tillinghast
Chase Twichell
Fred Viebahn
Ellen Bryant Voigt
Dan Wakefield
Derek Walcott
James Welch
Alan Williamson
Tobias Wolff
Al Young

PLOUGHSHARES, a journal of new writing, is guest-edited serially by prominent writers who explore different and personal visions, aesthetics, and literary circles. PLOUGHSHARES is published in April, August, and December at Emerson College, 100 Beacon Street, Boston, MA 02116-1596. Telephone: (617) 824-8753. Web address: www.emerson.edu/ploughshares.

EDITORIAL ASSISTANTS: Gregg Rosenblum, Melissa Cook, and Tom Herd.

POETRY READERS: Renee Rooks, Brian Scales, Michael Henry, Paul Berg, Charlotte Pence, Jessica Purdy, and Tom Laughlin.

FICTION READERS: Monique Hamzé, Tammy Zambo, Emily Doherty, Michael Rainho, Scott Clavenna, Karen Wise, Andrea Dupree, Jeffrey Freiert, Mary Jeanne Deery, Holly LeCraw Howe, Jessica Olin, Leah Stewart, Billie Lydia Porter, and Thomas McNeely.

SUBSCRIPTIONS (ISSN 0048-4474): $21 for one year (3 issues), $40 for two years (6 issues); $24 a year for institutions. Add $5 a year for international.

UPCOMING: Fall 1998, a fiction issue edited by Lorrie Moore, will appear in August 1998. Winter 1998–99, a poetry and fiction issue edited by Thomas Lux, will appear in December 1998.

SUBMISSIONS: Reading period is from August 1 to March 31 (postmark dates). Manuscripts sent from April to July are returned unread. Please see page 225 for detailed submission policies.

Classroom-adoption, back-issue, and bulk orders may be placed directly through PLOUGHSHARES. Authorization to photocopy journal pieces may be granted by contacting PLOUGHSHARES for permission and paying a fee of 5¢ per page, per copy. Microfilms of back issues may be obtained from University Microfilms. PLOUGHSHARES is also available as CD-ROM and full-text products from EBSCO, H.W. Wilson, Information Access, and UMI. Indexed in M.L.A. Bibliography, American Humanities Index, Index of American Periodical Verse, Book Review Index. Self-index through Volume 6 available from the publisher; annual supplements appear in the fourth number of each subsequent volume. The views and opinions expressed in this journal are solely those of the authors. All rights for individual works revert to the authors upon publication.

PLOUGHSHARES receives additional support from the Lannan Foundation and the Massachusetts Cultural Council.

Retail distribution by Bernhard DeBoer (Nutley, NJ), Ingram Periodicals (La Vergne, TN), and Koen Book Distributors (Moorestown, NJ).

Printed in the U.S.A. on recycled paper by Edwards Brothers.

© 1998 by Emerson College

CONTENTS

Spring 1998

Cover painting: *Birdies* by Christina Lanzl
Plaster, wax, and oil on paper, 20" x 15", 1993
Note: The cover image was digitally extended.
Courtesy of Elizabeth Baatz and Victor Maliar

Ploughshares Patrons

This nonprofit publication would not be possible without the support of our readers and the generosity of the following individuals and organizations.

COUNCIL
Denise and Mel Cohen
Eugenia Gladstone Vogel
Marillyn Zacharis

PATRONS
Anonymous
Jacqueline Liebergott
Estate of Charles T. Robb
Turow Foundation

FRIEND
In Memory of Larry Levis

ORGANIZATIONS
Emerson College
Lannan Foundation
Massachusetts Cultural Council

COUNCIL: $3,000 for two lifetime subscriptions, acknowledgement in the journal for three years, and votes on the Cohen and Zacharis Awards.
PATRON: $1,000 for a lifetime subscription and acknowledgement in the journal for two years.
FRIEND: $500 for a lifetime subscription and acknowledgement in the journal for one year.
All donations are tax-deductible.
Please make your check payable to
Ploughshares, Emerson College,
100 Beacon St., Boston, MA 02116.

STUART DYBEK

Introduction

A t the beginning of the process of reading fiction for this issue of *Ploughshares,* I worried briefly—foolishly—that I might not find enough stories to fill my allotted pages. Now, months later, my single regret is that I didn't have space for more of the fine work I had the opportunity to read.

One hears much lately about the problems that writers of literary work face: the bottom-line corporate climate of New York publishing houses; the tyrannical power of corporate bookstore chains; and the even more dire predictions that books—in fact, the printed word itself—will soon be obsolete. From that perspective these are bleak and threatening times for writers and readers of literary fiction.

But to my mind these are also tremendously exciting times in which to write. Writers, perhaps, to some degree, out of impatience with the compartmentalization one finds in academia and numerous writing programs, have stepped up the exploration of the borders between poetry and fiction, and fiction and nonfiction. Forms such as the short-short and the nonfiction novel are not only vehicles that allow for this, but symptoms of a deeper desire on the part of writers to situate themselves not in categories but along a fluid continuum—to be able to move Hermes-like through various literary dimensions.

I must confess that I thought about turning this issue into a forum on prose forms. I visualized a compendium of stories, tales, personal essays, meditations, memoirs, fables, prose poems, short-shorts, and, if possible, heretofore unnamed forms and anti-forms. (Perhaps, the short-short still belongs among the unnamed, as it's a cumbersome term that no one seems quite satisfied with. Grace Paley once quipped to me that short-short sounds more like a stammer than a literary form. Finding a label for them seems to demand nearly as much invention as writing them, and so we have sudden fictions, flash fictions, snap fictions, four-minute fictions. Two women students from the Warren Wilson program who studied with me took to referring to the short prose pieces they were writing as jockeys, and David Foster Wallace calls the short piece of his in this issue a nano-story.)

But as I began to read the fiction submitted to the magazine—I solicited only a small fraction of the work that appears here—I quickly discarded any leaning towards a particular agenda. Or, more accurately, I was quickly *seduced* away from programmatic notions. Seduced not just by the authentic mystery, the vibrant and sometimes gorgeous imagery, and the guileless wisdom that pervades these stories, but also by laughter. What a strange, all too rare, and welcome feeling to hear yourself, an audience of one, laughing uproariously in an echoey room. (The story I was reading was "Bad Jews," and, not content to remain an audience of one, I took it into my writing classes the next day to read aloud and shamelessly took the gratitude of my students' laughter as if *I* deserved it.)

As numerous prior guest editors of *Ploughshares* have inescapably remarked, I picked stories that moved me; stories that seemed to have compelled their authors to write them; stories that I thought were good—brilliant in some cases—and all of them beautiful.

A few more words by way of introduction on a couple of the pieces in this issue. The four short chapters by Kelly Simon are designed to function as what she calls independent "memory links"; they're excerpted from an unpublished book-length memoir.

"Islands," the story by A. Hemon, is one the earliest stories he's written in English. Mr. Hemon is Bosnian, and he settled in the United States, where he was traveling in 1992, when the war in Bosnia prevented his return. He wrote "Islands" in the spring of 1995, after enduring a three-year period in which he found that he could no longer write fiction in his native language, but could not write yet in English, either.

JANE HIRSHFIELD

Introduction

What is the meaning of a "little" magazine in the life of poetry in American culture today? Is it a forum for the inquisitive reader to see what is being written, what kinds of thoughts and forms of thought are occupying the minds and hearts of writers both established and unknown? Is it a place for those writers to put their work forward first to the doorkeeping editors, then to readers—a kind of gladiatorial testing ground, perhaps? Is it, as the deconstructionists might propose, a locus for the prevailing cultural tendencies of mind and style to impose themselves further, or, as the experimentalist avant-garde might propose, a place where the marginal can find a small space in which to be heard, to wedge a clearing amid established patterns of speech and of being?

These are real questions, even interesting ones, but they are also tired ones. I will confess that when opening the envelopes of poems sent on to me by the unfailingly gracious staff of *Ploughshares*, I did not consider my activity as guest editor a chance to impose or explore any theory of art and culture. I did not consider the role of the words I read in regard to the culture at large. I did not consider the role of "poetry," or whether or not it "matters." I did not consider—though I did notice—the way certain themes and types of poems recurred from submission to submission. What I considered was the poems: the words on the page, and the effect they had on my heart and mind and body as I let them enter my being. And what I hoped for, each time I turned to a fresh page, was nothing less than to find myself moved and transformed.

Make no mistake: I consider such a moment of transformation a radical event. Radical in both senses of the word—an extraordinary poem requires of its reader a fundamental revolution in being, and also returns the reader to some deep root of being which has been present in us from the start. It may be that both senses are necessary for our survival: we live so much of the time in a state of estrangement from ourselves. Estranged from the possibility of a real knowledge of our own experience, estranged from our own hearts, we wander the hours and years in a kind of day-blindness, lost in the alleyways of an expected life. It is easier, certainly, to navigate a life we believe is predictable, is knowable, is known. And the costs? Bearable—until some event forces us to realize it has all been a dream, a falseness, and we must recover the ability to see not what we wish to see, but what is: a wholly surprising world.

A good poem offers always some entrance into and reminder of the fact that genuine experience is unexpected. A good poem shocks us awake, one way or another—through its beauty, its insight, its music, it shakes or seduces the reader out of the common gaze and into a genuine looking. It breaks the sleepwalking habit in our eyes, in our ears, in our mouths, and sets us adrift in a small raft under a vast night-sky of stars. We feel ourselves moving, too, above a vast, cold-streaming current carrying inner-lit sea creatures, tangles of kelp strands, fishes. Thus we learn the deep clefts of the mid-ocean land-rifts; thus the wave-blanketed mountains rise up before us as islands, a new habitation for heart and mind.

We depart the known ease in order to arrive somewhere other than where we were. We travel by poem, as by any other means, in order to see for ourselves more than was seen.

The record of those travels matters—one person's word-wakened knowledge becomes another's. We seed poems into magazines, into books, onto the Internet, over the radio, whether to be met by two million people or two hundred, because we are beings who learn from one another how to become our full selves. The pages of *Ploughshares*, filled year by year with new poems and new stories chosen by new selectors, matter to me immensely because on any of them I may meet the few words that will suddenly cast me into a widened humanness, a widened knowledge and range of being.

This encounter of words and reader occurs in privacy, in silence; if any of these pages becomes such a moment of liberation for any of its readers, it is unlikely that I or the words' author will ever hear of it. Yet I have utter confidence that the sum of such moments is one of the essential ways that both individuals and cultures move forward—into awakening; into first the recognition of and then responsibility for our kinship with others; into agreement that this life in all its harshness and beauty is one we want not merely to get through blindly, but make our own. And so we say of a good poem, of a good story, "powerful."

Recently, Czeslaw Milosz mentioned to me his theory that Walt Whitman was responsible for the First World War. "You see," he said, "by the end of the nineteenth century, Whitman began to be widely translated, and all the young revolutionaries of Europe read eagerly and took to heart this new cry for democratic being…" Then there is the letter I once received from a woman who had read *The Ink Dark Moon:* "I heard in those ancient poems what was missing from my life, and ended my marriage." I remember, too, my own return from a period of prolonged depression, a dark hibernation of being; after months of not reading anything, I found one voice I could tolerate—Rilke's. Slowly, surely, his intimate, inward murmuring guided me back to the terrifying shoals of aliveness.

I offer this powerful and dangerous thing into your hands, a "little" magazine. It has been a pleasure to be part of its coming into existence.

Islands

1

We got up at dawn, ignored the yolky sun, loaded our navy-blue Austin with suitcases, and then drove straight to the coast, stopping only on the verge of Sarajevo, so I could pee. I sang communist songs the entire journey: songs about mournful mothers looking through graves for their dead sons; songs about the revolution, steaming and steely, like a locomotive; songs about striking miners burying their dead comrades. By the time we got to the coast, I had almost lost my voice.

2

We waited for the ship on a long stone pier, which burnt the soles of my feet as soon as I took off my sandals. The air was sweltering, saturated with sea-ozone, exhaustion, and the smell of coconut sun-lotion, coming from the German tourists, already red and shellacked, lined up for a photo at the end of the pier. We saw the thin stocking of smoke on the horizon-thread, then the ship itself, getting bigger, slightly slanted sideways, like a child's drawing. I had a round straw hat with all the seven dwarfs painted on it. It threw a short, dappled shadow over my face. I had to raise my head to look at the grown-ups. Otherwise, I would look at their gnarled knees, the spreading sweat-stains on their shirts and sagging wrinkles of fat on their thighs. One of the Germans, an old, bony man, got down on his knees and then puked over the pier edge. The vomit hit the surface and then dispersed in different directions, like children running away to hide from the seeker. Under the wave-throbbing ochre and maroon island of vomit, a school of aluminum fish gathered and nibbled it peevishly.

3

The ship was decrepit, with peeling steel stairs and thin leaves of rust that could cut your fingers on the handrails. The staircase wound upwards like a twisted towel. "Welcome," said an unshaven man, in a T-shirt picturing a boat with a smoke-snake wobbling on the waves and, above it, the sun with a U-smile and the umlaut of eyes. We sat on the upper board and the ship leapt over humble waves, panting and belching. We passed a line of little islands, akin to car wrecks by the road, and I would ask my parents, "Is this Mljet?" and they would say, "No." From behind one of the islands, shaven by a wild fire, a gust of waylaying wind attacked us, snatched the straw hat off my head and tossed it into the sea. I watched the hat teetering away, my hair pressed against my skull, like a helmet, and I understood that I would never, ever see it again. I wished to go back in time and hold on to my hat before the surreptitious whirlwind would hit me in the face again. The ship sped away from the hat, and the hat was transformed into a distant beige stain on the snot-green sea. I began crying and sobbed myself to sleep. When I woke up, the ship was docked and the island was Mljet.

4

Uncle Julius impressed a stern, moist kiss on my cheek--the corner of his mouth touched the corner of my mouth, leaving a dot of spit above my lip. But his lips were soft, like slugs, as if there was nothing behind to support them. As we walked away from the pier, he told us that he forgot his teeth at home, and then, so as to prove that he was telling us the truth, he grinned at me, showing me his pink gums with cinnabar scars. He reeked of pine cologne, but a whiff redolent of rot and decay escaped his insides and penetrated the cologne cloud. I hid my face into my mother's skirt. I heard his snorting chuckle. "Can we please go back home!" I cried.

5

We walked up a sinuous road exuding heat. Uncle Julius's sandals clattered in a tranquilizing rhythm and I felt sleepy. There was a dense, verdureless thicket alongside the road. Uncle Julius told us that there used to be so many poisonous snakes on Mljet that people used to walk in tall rubber boots all the time, even at home, and snake bites were as common as mosquito bites. Everybody used to know how to slice off the bitten piece of flesh in a split second, before the venom could spread. Snakes killed chickens and dogs. Once, he said, a snake was attracted by the scent of milk, so it curled up on a sleeping baby. And then someone heard of the mongoose, how it kills snakes with joy, and they sent a man to Africa and he brought a brood of mongooses and they let them loose on the island. There were so many snakes that it was like a paradise for them. You could walk for miles and hear nothing but the hissing of snakes and the shrieks of mongooses and the bustle and rustle in the thicket. But then mongooses killed all the snakes and bred so much that the island became too small for them. Chickens started disappearing, cats also, there were rumors of rabid mongooses and some even talked about monster mongooses that were the result of paradisiacal inbreeding. Now they were trying to figure out how to get rid of mongooses. "So that's how it is," he said, "it's all one pest after another, like revolutions. Life is nothing if not a succession of evils," he said, and then stopped and took a pebble out of his left sandal. He showed the puny, gray pebble to us, as if holding unquestionable evidence that he was right.

6

He opened the gate and we walked through a small, orderly garden with stout tomato stalks, like sentries, alongside the path. His wife stood in the courtyard, her face like a loaf of bread with a small tubby potato in the middle, arms akimbo, her calves full of bruises and blood vessels on the verge of bursting, ankles swollen. She was barefoot, her big toes were crooked, taking a sudden turn, as if backing away in disgust from each other. She enveloped my head with her palms, twisted my head upwards, and then put her mouth over my mouth, leaving a thick layer of warm saliva, which I hastily wiped off with my shoulder. Aunt Lyudmila was her name.

7

I clambered, dragging a bag full of plastic beach toys, after my sprightly parents, up a concrete staircase on the side of the house, with sharp stair edges and pots of unconcerned flowers, like servants with candles, on the banister side.

8

The room was fragrant with lavender, mosquito-spray poison, and clean, freshly ironed bedsheets. There was an aerial picture of a winding island (Mljet, it said in the lower right corner) and a picture of Comrade Tito, smiling, black-and-white, on the opposite wall. Below the window, the floor was dotted with mosquitoes—with a large green-glittering fly or a bee here and there—still stricken by the surprise. When I moved towards them, the wisp caused by my motion made them ripple away from me, as if retreating, wary of another surprise.

9

I lay on the bed, listening to the billowing-curtain flaps, looking at the picture of Mljet. There were two oblong lakes, touching each other, at the top end of the picture-island, and on one of those lakes there was an island.

10

I woke up and the night was rife with the cicada hum, perpetual, as if it were the hum of the island engine. They were all sitting outside, around the table underneath the shroud of vine twisting up the lattice. There was a long-necked carafe, full of black wine, in the center of the table, like an axis. Uncle Julius was talking and they all laughed. He would bulge his eyes, lean forward, he would thrust his fist forward, then open it, and the hand would have the index finger pointed at the space between my mother and his wife, and then the hand would retract back into the fist, but the finger would reappear, tapping its tip against the table, as if telegraphing a message. He would then stop talking and withdraw back into the starting position, and he would just watch them as they were laughing.

11

Uncle Julius spoke: "We brought beekeeping to Bosnia. Before the Ukrainians came, the natives kept their bees in mud-and-straw hives and when they wanted the honey they would just kill them all with sulfur. My grandfather had fifty beehives three years after coming to Bosnia. Before he died, he was sick for a long time. And the day he died, he asked to be taken to the bees and they took him there. He sat by the hives for hours, and wept and wept, and wept out a sea of tears, and then they put him back into his bed and an hour later he died."

"What did he die of?" Aunt Lyudmila asked.

"Dysentery. People used to die of that all the time. They'd just shit themselves to death."

12

I went down the stairs and declared my thirst. Aunt Lyudmila walked over to the dark corner on my right-hand side, turned on the light ablaze, and there was a concrete box with a large square wooden lid. She took off the lid and grabbed a tin cup and shoved her arm into the square. I went to the water tank (for that's what it really was) and peeked over. I saw a white slug, as big as my father's thumb, on the opposite wall. I could not tell whether it was moving upwards or it was just frozen by our sudden presence. The dew on its back twinkled, it looked like a severed tongue. I glanced at Aunt Lyudmila, but she didn't seem to have noticed anything. She offered me the cup, but I shook my head and refused to drink the water, which, besides, appeared turbid.

So they brought me a slice of cold watermelon and I drowsily masticated it. "Look at yourself," Uncle Julius said. "You don't want to drink the water! What would you do if you were so thirsty that you were nearly crazy and having one thought only—water, water!—and there's no water? How old are you?" "Nine," my mother said.

13

Uncle Julius told us that when he was in the Arkhangelsk camp, Stalin and his parliament devised a law that said if you were repeatedly late for school or missed several days with no excuse, you would get six months to three years in a camp. So, suddenly, in 1943, the camp was full of children, only a little bit older than me—twelve, fifteen years old. They didn't know what to do in the camp, so the criminals took the nicest looking to their quarters and fed them and, you know (no, I didn't), abused them. So they were there. They died like flies, because it was cold, and they lost their warm clothing, they didn't know how to preserve or protect the scarce food and water they were allotted. Only the ones that had protectors were able to survive. And there was a boy named Vanyka: gaunt, about twelve, blond, blue eyes. He survived by filching food from the weaker ones, by lending himself to different protectors and bribing guards. Once—I think he drank some

vodka with the criminals—he started shouting: "Thank you,
Vozhd, for my happy childhood!" From the top of his lungs:
"Thank you, Stalin, for my happy childhood!" And they beat him
with gun butts and took him away.

14

"Don't torture the boy with these stories. He won't be able to
sleep ever again."
"No, let him hear, he should know."

15

Then they sent Uncle Julius to a different camp, and then to
another one, and he didn't even know how much time or how
many camps he passed through, and he found himself in Siberia.
One spring, his job was to dig big graves in the thawing ground,
take the dead to the grave on a large cart, and then stuff them into
the grave. Fifty per grave was the prescribed amount. Sometimes
he had to stamp on the top of the graveload to get more space and
meet the plan. He had big, big boots. One day they told him that
there was a dead man in solitary confinement, so he pushed his
cart there and put the corpse on the cart, and as he was pushing,
the corpse moaned: "Let me die! Let me die!" I was so scared I
almost died, I fell down, and he kept moaning: "Let me die! I don't
want to live!" So I pushed the cart behind the barrack and I leaned
over him. He was emaciated and had no teeth and one of his ears
was missing, but he had blue, blue eyes. It was Vanyka! He looked
much older, oh my God! So I gave him a piece of bread that I had
saved for the bad days and told him that I remembered him and
this is what he told me.

16

They took him away and mauled him for days and did all sorts
of things to him. Then they moved him to another camp and he
had problems there all the time, because he would speak out
again, despite his better judgment. He knew how to steal from the
weaker and there were still men who liked him. He won acclaim
when he killed a marked person, some Jew, after losing a card
game. He killed more. He did bad, bad things and learned how to
survive, but he could never keep his snout shut. So they sent him

to the island where they kept the worst of the worst. The nearest guard was on the shore fifty kilometers away. They let the inmates rob and kill each other like mad dogs. Once a month the guards would come in, leave the food, and count the corpses and graves and go back to their barracks by the sea. So one day Vanyka and two others killed some other inmates, took their food and clothes, and set out on foot towards the shore. It was a very, very cold winter—pines would crack like matches every day—so they thought they could walk over the frozen strait, if they avoided the guards. But they got lost and ran out of food and Vanyka and one of the other two agreed by exchanging glances to kill the third one. And they did and they ate his flesh, and they walked and walked and walked. Then Vanyka killed the other one and ate him. But the guards with dogs tracked him down and caught him and he ended up in solitary confinement here and he didn't know how long he had been there. All he wanted was to die and he'd smash his head against the walls and he'd try to choke himself with his tongue. He refused to eat, but they'd force him, if only to make him live longer and suffer more. "Let me die!" he cried and cried.

17

Uncle Julius was reticent and no one dared to say anything. But I asked: "So what happened to him?"

"He was killed," he said, making a motion with his hand, as if thrusting me aside, out of his sight.

18

I woke up and didn't know where I was or who I was, but then I saw the photo of Mljet and I recognized it. I got up, out of my non-being, and stepped into the inchoate day. It was purblindingly bright, but I could hear the din of the distant beach: bashful whisper of waves, echoes of sourceless music, warbling of boat motors, shrieks of children, syncopated splashing of oars. Bees levitated over the staircase flowers and I passed them cautiously. There was breakfast on the table in the net-like shadow of the vines: a plate with smoldering, soggy eggs, a cup with a stream of steam rushing upwards, and seven slices of bread, on a mirroring steel tray, leaning on each other like fallen dominoes. There was no one around, apart from shadows stretching on the courtyard stone pavement. I sat down and stirred my white coffee. There was a dead bee in the whirl and it kept revolving on its back, slower and slower, until it came to a reluctant stop.

19

After breakfast, we would go down a dirt path resembling a long burrow in the shrub. I'd carry my blue and white Nivea inflatable ball and sometimes I would inadvertently drop it and it would bounce, ahead of us, in slow motion. I'd hear bustle in the thicket—a snake, perhaps. But then there would be more bustle and I'd imagine a mongoose killing the snake, the whole bloody battle, the writhing snake entangled with the mongoose trying to bite off its head, just the way I saw on TV, on *Survival.* I'd wait for my parents, for I didn't know what sort of feeling a fierce mongoose would have towards a curious boy—would it, perhaps, want to bite his head off?

20

We'd get to the gravel beach, near the dam dividing the two lakes. I'd have to sit on the towel for a while before I would be allowed to swim. On the left, there would usually be an old man, his skin puckered here and there, a spy novel over his face, white hair meekly bristling on his chest, his belly nearly imperceptibly ascending and descending, with a large metallic-green fly on the brim of his navel. On our right, two symmetrical old men, with straw hats, in baggy trunks, would play chess in serene silence, with their doughy breasts overlooking the board. There were three children a little farther away. They would sit on the towel, gathered around a woman, probably their mother, who would distribute tomatoes and slices of bread with a layer of sallow spread on them. The children would all simultaneously bite into their slices and their tomatoes, and then chew vigorously. The tomato slime would drip down their chins, they would be seemingly unperturbed, but when they were done eating, the mother would wipe their recalcitrant faces with a stained white rag.

21

Finally, my parents would tell me I could swim and I'd totter over the painful gravel and enter the shallows. I would see throbbing jellyfish floating by. The rocks at the bottom were covered with slimy, slippery lichen. I'd hesitantly dive and the shock of coldness would make me feel present in my own body—I'd be clearly aware of my ends, I'd be aware that my skin was the border between the world and me. Then I'd stand up, the quivering lake up to my nipples, and I'd wave to my parents and they'd shout: "Five more minutes!"

22

Sometimes I'd see fish in pellucid water, gliding along the bottom. Once I saw a school of fish that looked like miniature swordfish, with silver bellies and pointed needle noses. They were all moving as one and then they stopped before me, and hundreds of little wide-open eyes stared at me in dreadful surprise. Then I blinked and they flitted away.

23

We walked up the path as the sun was setting. Everything attained a brazen shade and, now and then, there would be a thin gilded beam, which managed to break through the shrub and olive trees, like a spear, sticking out of the ground. Cicadas were revving and the warmth of the ground enhanced the fragrance of dry pine needles on the path. I entered the stretch of the path that had been in the shadow of the tall pines for a while, and the sudden coolness made me conscious of how hot my shoulders felt. I pressed my thumb firmly against my shoulder and, when I lifted it, a pallid blot appeared, then it slowly shrunk, back into the ruddiness.

24

There was a man holding a German shepherd on a leash, much of which was coiled around his hand. The shepherd was attempting to jump at a mongoose backed against a short ruin of a stone wall. As the dog's jaw snapped a breath away from the mongoose's snout, the man would pull the dog back. The mongoose's hair bristled up, and it grinned to show its teeth, appearing dangerous, but I knew it was just madly scared. The eyes had a red glow, akin to the glow that people who glanced at the flashlight have on bad color photos. The dog was growling and barking and I saw the pink and brown gums and the bloodthirst saliva running down the sides of the jaw. Then the man let the dog go and there was, for just a moment, hissing and wheezing, growling and shrieking. The man pulled the dog back and the mongoose lay on its back, showing its teeth in a useless scowl, the paws spread, as if showing it was harmless now, and the eyes were wide open, the irises stretched to the edge of the pupils, flabbergasted. There was a hole in its chest—the dog seemed to have bitten off a part of it—and I saw the heart, like a tiny tomato, pulsating, as if hiccuping, slower and slower, with slightly longer moments between the throbs, and it simply stopped.

25

We walked through the dusk. My sandals were full of pine needles and I would have to stop to take them out. Thousands of fireflies floated in the shrubs, lighting and vanishing, as if they were hidden fairy photographers with flashlights, taking our snapshots. "Are you hungry?" my mother asked.

26

We would sit under the cloak of vines, with a rotund jar of limpid honey and a plate of pickles. Uncle Julius would dip a pickle into the honey and several bees would peel themselves off the jar and hover above the table. I would dip my finger and try to get it to my lips before the thinning thread of honey would drip on my naked thighs, but I would never make it.

Sometimes, around lunchtime, Uncle Julius would take me to his apiary. He would put on a white overall and a white hat with a veil falling down on his chest, so he looked like a bride. He would light a torn rag and order me to hold it, so as to repel the bees. He would tell me to be absolutely silent and not to move and not to blink. I'd peek from behind his back, my hand with the smoldering rag protruded. He would take the lid off a beehive, carefully, as if he were afraid of awakening the island, and the buzz would rise like a cloud of dust and hover around us. He would scrape off the wax between the frames and then take them out, one by one, and show them to me. I'd see the molasses of bees fidgeting. "They work all the time," he'd whisper. "They never stop." I'd be frightened by the possibility of being stung, even though he told me that the bees would not attack me if I pretended not to exist.

The fear would swell, and the more I'd think about it, the more unbearable the unease would be. Eventually, I'd break down and run back to the house, get on the stairs, from where I'd see him, remote, immobile, apart from the slow, wise motions of his apt hands. I'd watch him, as if he were projected on a screen of olive trees and isles of beehives, then he'd turn to me and I could discern a peculiar, tranquil smile behind the veil.

27

Mother and Father were sitting at the stern, with their feet in tepid bilge water, Uncle Julius was rowing, and I was sitting at the prow, my feet dangling overboard. The surface of the lake would ascend with an inconspicuous wave and my feet would delve into the coolness of menthol-green water. With the adagio of oars, creaking and splashing, we glissaded towards the lake island. There was a dun-colored stone building, with small drawn-in windows, and an array of crooked olive trees in front of it. Uncle Julius steered the scow toward a puny desolate pier. I slipped stepping out, but Uncle Julius grabbed my hand and I hung for a moment over the throbbing lake with a sodden loaf of bread and an ardently smiling woman on a magazine page stuck to the surface, like an ice floe.

28

"These lakes," Uncle Julius said, "used to be a pirate haven in the sixteenth century. They'd hoard the loot and bring hostages here and kill them and torture them—in this very building—if they didn't get the ransom. They say that this place is still haunted by the ghosts of three children they hung on meat hooks because their parents didn't pay the ransom. Then this was a nunnery and some people used to believe that even the nuns were not nuns but witches. Then it was a German prison. And now, mind you, it's a hotel, but there are hardly any tourists ever."

29

We walked into the sonorous chill of a large stone-walled hall. There was a reception desk, but nobody behind it, and a smiling Tito picture over the numbered cubbyhole shelf. Then we walked through a long tunnel and then through a low door, so everyone but me had to bow their heads, then we were in a cubicle-like windowless room ("This used to be a nun cell," Uncle Julius whispered), then we entered the eatery (they had to bend their knees and bow their heads, as if genuflecting, again) with long wooden tables and, on them, two parallel rows of plates and utensils. We sat there waiting for the waiter. There was a popsicle-yellow lizard, as big as a new pencil, on the stone wall behind Uncle Julius's back. It looked at us with an unblinking marble eye, apparently perplexed, and then it scurried upwards, towards an obscure window.

30

This was what Uncle Julius told us:

"When I was a young student in Moscow, in the thirties, I saw the oldest man in the world. I was in a biology class, it was in a gigantic amphitheater, hundreds of rows, thousands of students. They brought in an old man who couldn't walk, so two comrades carried him and he had his arms over their shoulders. His feet were dangling between them, but he was all curled up like a baby. They said he was a hundred and fifty-eight years old and somewhere from the Caucasus. They put him sideways on the desk and he started crying like a baby, so they gave him a stuffed toy—a cat, I think, but I can't be certain, because I was sitting all the way up in one of the last aisles. I was looking at him as if through the wrong side of a telescope. And the teacher told us that the old man cried all the time, ate only liquid foods, and couldn't bear being separated from his favorite toy. The teacher said that he slept a lot, didn't know his name, and had no memories. He could say only a couple of words, like water, poo-poo, and such. I figured out then that life is a circle, you get back right where you started if you get to be a hundred and fifty-eight years old. It's like a dog chasing its own tail, all is for naught. We live and live, and in the end we're just like this boy"—he pointed at me—"knowing nothing, remembering nothing. You might as well stop living now, my son. You might just as well stop, for nothing will change."

31

When I woke up, after a night of unsettling dreams, the suitcases were agape and my parents were packing them with wrinkled underwear and shirts. Uncle Julius came up with a jar of honey as big as my head and gave it to my father. He looked at the photo of Mljet and then put the tip of his finger at the point in the upper right corner, near the twin lakes, which looked like gazing eyes. "We are here," he said.

32

The sun had not risen yet from behind the hill, so there were no shadows and everything looked muffled, as if under a sheet of fine gauze. We walked down the narrow road and the asphalt was cold and moist. We passed a man carrying a cluster of dead fish, with the hooks in their carmine gills. He said "Good morning!" and smiled.

We waited at the pier. A shabby boat, with paint falling off and *Pirate* written in pale letters on the bow, was heading, coughing, towards the open sea. A man with an anchor tattooed on his right arm was standing at the rudder. He had a torn red and black flannel shirt, black soccer shorts, and no shoes—his feet bloated and filthy. He was looking straight ahead towards the ferry that was coming into the harbor. The ferry slowed down to the point of hesitant floating, and then it dropped down its entrance door, like a castle bridge, with a harsh peal. It was a different ship than the ship we had come on, but the same man with the hobbling-boat shirt said "Welcome!" again, and smiled, as if recognizing us.

We passed the same islands. They were like heavy molded loaves of bread, dropped behind a gigantic ship. On one of the islands, and we passed it close-by, there was a herd of goats. They looked at us mildly confounded, and then, one by one, lost interest and returned to grazing. A man with a camera, probably a German tourist, took a picture of the goats, and then gave the camera to his speckle-faced, blue-eyed son. The boy pointed the camera towards the sun, but the man jokingly admonished him, turning him, and the camera, towards us, while we grinned at him, helpless.

33

It took us only four hours to get home from the coast and I slept all the time, oblivious to the heat, until we reached Sarajevo. When we got home, the shriveled plants and flowers were in the midst of the setting-sun orange spill. All the plants had withered, because the neighbor who was supposed to water them died of a sudden heart attack. The cat, having not been fed for more than a week, was emaciated and nearly mad with hunger. I would call her, but she wouldn't come to me, she would just look at me with irreversible hatred.

AL YOUNG

Landscape Mode

Overlooking the Cumberland River,
Clarksville, Tennessee,
early November 1996

In ancient Chinese paintings we see more sky than
earth, so when clouds hurry by in silver-gray
inkbursts of rolling readiness right along the river,

ripe with rain, rushing the road of time along,
pushing back light, belittling the black and white clarity
of Hollywood in its prime, the eye climbs down to greet

with shining gusto trees along the shore, Opryland
beyond the frame, the blue horizon hidden in a sea
of possibilities. And beyond this there's jazz: Jimmy Giuffre's

"Train on the River" stretched out strong like a pet cat
—and that's that. But not quite. This poem paints
poorly what sketchers and colorists do best. The rest

should come out empty, allowing you to fill in your own
basic emptiness, your openness, your self-portrait
forged and catalogued; on quiet exhibit, on temporary loan.

Descended from clouds immensely more ancient than China,
you never quit becoming the background, the field in a sky
whose subtle earthiness sails over our heads altogether.

ROBERT WRIGLEY

Ice Fishing

From open water at the lake's
unfrozen outlet, steam rises, a scrim
dim enough to turn the sun as round as a dime,

though it's still so bright across snow,
so low in the sky it rings
with a ball-peen clang behind his eyes,

each time he looks up
from his augured hole in the ice.
Wind spins a spider-silk filament

of frost from the dorsal fin of a quick frozen
blueblack, and blood spots
the snow around the hole.

From the darkening woods
two coyotes pipe and prate, the late
mouse they toss aloft in play, the same

they'll squabble over soon. And soon
the sun will sink an edge in the ridge,
and the wind will chase its tail

behind the trees. Then the man will stand
and take his stool and the tool
for the ice and the tool

for the fish and the fish and leave.
Only the low, late coals of his fire left behind,
pinkening down toward pure black ash,

the dark below blowing a kiss to the night,
the hole scabbing over already with ice,
by the blood-freckled cheek of the evening snow.

Cargo

You have seen vines climbing
themselves, as though the moon
were riding inside.
                        Hordes
of ants scooting along one spot
and then scooting back again,
sporting banners many times
their size of butterfly wings.

Consider an unruly nation,
a revolution gathering forces,
like this body of yours, wholly
politic.
              In its momentary
congress, each cell, dedicated
to its way, chitters as it
chambles.
                    Devouring the world
in passing, it is soon devoured
in turn, the moonlit mouths
already well along inside it.

Thoreau and the Crickets

He found them bedded in ice, in the frozen puddles
　　Among reeds and clumps of sedges in the marsh:
　　　　House and field crickets lying near the surface
On their sides or upside down, their brittle hind legs
　　Cocked as if to jump as free as fiddlers
　　　　In the final rain before winter. The ice
Had clarified the brown and green shades
　　Of their chitin and magnified
　　　　The thickened radiant veins of the forewings
On which they'd made their music
　　Those nights when he'd listened, half-asleep,
　　　　To their creaking, their wise old saws
That told him over and over they were with him
　　And of him down to the vibrant depths
　　　　Of his eardrums and canals and the foundation
Of his house on earth. With his heels and hands
　　He broke the puddles around them carefully,
　　　　Cracking them loose and filling his coat pockets
With fragments like clear glass, holding them hard
　　As fossils in shale. He would take them home
　　　　And learn from them, examine their lost lives
With scales and ruler, tweezers and microscope.
　　He would bring them back to order and pay homage
　　　　To all they'd been and left undone. He strode
Briskly and happily through the crusted lanes
　　And slipped through the paths of town, delighted
　　　　To be alive all winter, to be ready
And able to warm their spirits with his own,
　　But on his doorstep, reaching into his coat,
　　　　He lifted out, dripping with snow-melt,
Two hands full of wriggling, resurrected crickets
　　Crawling over each other, waving and flexing
　　　　Antennae and stiff legs to search his palms

For another springtime. For a while, he held them
   And watched them wriggle drunkenly
      And scrabble in half-death for what they imagined
He had to give, then put them gently
   Again into his pockets and carried them
      Back through the snow and ice to their cold beds.

Entering

The passengers riding the train
do not know. Nor do
the taxi drivers
lining up
miles away. But they trust
they will meet each other.
The yellow cabs
inch forward
like the hours of a life.
Each time a door opens,
someone enters.

White Wall

*"I've decided the only thing that really interests me
is how the sun hits a white wall."*
—Edward Hopper to Andrew Wyeth

Somehow the crow snuck in, its caws echo
      in the fluorescence of the hallways.

We are all waiting at the ICU ward
      for your suffering to come to an end.

Tonight the full moon casts long shadows
      against the hospital wall. Lung cancer

has spread fast, the x-rays show
      the luminous bunches of grapes inside

your lungs. Within an hour of ruckus—
      between beeps, ticks, bleeps—all those

white noises only discernable to the sick,
      the heart races to be nourished, first

by articles & prepositions (tell a little
      lie, call it a Cuba libre), next feed

on the adverbs & adjectives, no
      need now for conjunctions. Leave

the verbs for last, that final option
      as the morphine works its magic,

pain held at bay for now. Out beyond
      the buoys, beyond where the opaline

turns to emerald green, an island
    emerges, the island of your birth.

Listen, now, a *cotorra* cries out.
    Your soul wants to make a quiet

entrance and take its place among
    the *ceibas, framboyan,* and *palmeras,*

between the diamond dust sand
    and the luscious foliage. The wind

announces your presence. Rest now;
    rest finally. A rain falls and washes

memory away to become a new seed,
    a sprout, a jungle, a man born infant.

But we return to this business
    of white walls, the crow cassocked

in its vestibule of bleakness, blinded
    by the hocus-pocus of the end

of the millennium. Inside penumbra,
    the ebb of weak light confronts

the shadows upon the once white wall.
    Your heart pulse rattles in your ears:

"*Tienes dolor, Papi,*" a nurse wants
    to know. Inside the morphine drip,

the sound of waves beckons you back,
    then the sound of something hitting

an oxygen tank, becomes the pealing
    of bells. Who stand privy to the mystery

of the concave? The women angels
        come to grip your hands which remain

bound up so you won't tug the tubes
        of the respirator. Next door they ready

a man for his third and possibly final
        surgery; his gut busted and the infection

is killing him. Who returns from such
        journeys? Your glazed eyes look

beyond the ceiling at the black buzzards
        (crows?) circling the sky. The veins

under the thin skin of your temples knot,
        you speak by knitting your brows,

batting your eyelids, you speak loudest
        with the bleeping of your heart monitor.

No words left to describe all the qualities
        of a white wall. Thus arrives the hour

of great stillness when the distant coastal
        lights flicker down to a slow beat

on the water's surface. The heart
        shimmers, its beat finds solace in the way

the moon casts long shadows against
a white wall—not merely enough suffices in the end.

With Sam

Photo of Beckett on the fridge.
He and I, smoke. All three
of us are humming. A gust
twitches the plastic wedge
covering the kitchen window.
I see a neighbor at tai chi,
posing like Giacometti's tree.
Latched to his hand, Sam's
cigarette is a sixth digit.
From down the block we hear
a child's voice, yelling at—
"Bad, bad, very, very, bad."
Autumn; winter exudes the air.
I boil water. The thing to do.
Sam smokes. I light one, too.
With all this...elongation,
I don't wish to appear rude.

KAY RYAN

Mockingbird

Nothing whole
is so bold,
we sense. Nothing
not cracked is
so exact and
of a piece. He's
the distempered
emperor of parts,
the king of patch,
the master of
pastiche, who so
hashes other birds'
laments, so minces
their capriccios that
the dazzle of dispatch
displaces the originals.
As though brio really
does beat feeling,
the way two aces beat
three hearts when it's
cards you're dealing.

Corners

All but saints
and hermits
mean to paint
themselves
toward an exit

leaving a
pleasant ocean
of azure or jonquil
ending neatly
at the doorsill.

But sometimes
something happens:

a minor dislocation
by which the doors
and windows
undergo a
small rotation
to the left a little

but repeatedly.
It isn't
obvious immediately.

Only toward evening
and from the
farthest corners
of the houses
of the painters

comes a chorus
of individual keening
as of kenneled dogs
someone is mistreating.

LIZ ROSENBERG

Fathomless: The Interview

How do you sleep? he asked,
and I said Wait—I know—
because I didn't know.
My husband insists
I sleep a certain way.
—Not on your stomach?
He seemed disappointed. Then on your back?
—Maybe, my back, or my side.
I didn't tell him, I sleep like something
tossed
onshore, —or the way we are taught
the infant cherubs sleep, sideways,
with prayerful hands tucked up—
My son sleeps this way,
and we are very much alike.
I didn't return the question.
Doctor, how do *you* sleep?
Which letter does your body form
in the bedroom, reaching out
for whose embrace? But I picture him
nonetheless, asking questions, turning
and groping in the fathomless dark.

As Is

No one is awake yet, neither the cardinals who live
           in the gnarled, rotted-out
apple tree, nor Lucy my younger daughter whose shrieks are

        our alarm and birdsong.
This is the best hour, neither night nor morning, a place
          in which shadows

become more real than the things that cast them.
        "Premature atrial contractions,"
said the ER doctor, barely glancing at my "strip," my heart's

        poor penmanship,
which he showed me with mild reproof. My hand coaxing
         invisible words

from this white paper is turning to shadow more quickly
         than I can write
its transformation down. My pulse flutters.

        Yesterday the blue jay
in our cat's mouth, and I stop mid-sentence to remember
        the tremor of the blue, black-barred

wings, its punk-rocker head held fast between
         incisors, and the cat
with her gorgeous tortoise-shell markings, three black whiskers

        among the white,
and her hypnotic neon-green eyes, who brought the bird
        to our back door to show us.

Yesterday death stalked and caught, then opened her mouth
         to mew, and the bird
flew in a blue flash into the sixty-foot pine and shrieked

         back at its mortality,
now circling the tall tree. The other birds started scolding too.
         "No one's heartbeat is ever

perfectly regular. Dial 911 if you start to fibrillate
         or your heart
stops." Thanks, Doc. Thank you, daylight, that seeps

         through the slats of the blinds
I raise to see the world come back—leaves of the magnolia that dawn
         varnishes, the twisted

basketball hoop and backboard on a rusted steel pole blown over
         by Hurricane Opal,
our half-blighted pear tree, black leaves

         among the first greeny-white
blossoms the wind blows to the ground in flurries of snow
         that will take all

this still cold March day to melt, and the litter of light
         caught in the broken glass
along the curb. Hard frost has silvered

         the grass so each blade
is an illuminated letter in the manuscript I'll read forever
         and never understand.

I count my resting pulse, black beads of the blood's
         rosary that the body
tells over and over. How does one live

on the faultline, the crack
in the heart's bedrock? God, you are seismic. Your will
          is the Richter scale.

Though you tear me down and shatter whatever
          roof I raise,
I do not want another life. Give me

          this one morning, a single
entry in the year's dream diary, and let it be "as is"—
          meaning "no guarantee

against the transmission falling out" in the OK Used Car Lot
          salesman's lingo.
As is, the bird I can't identify, who quavers

          vee-ur, vee-ur
as if to say it's all right that things repeat themselves,
          that the sun rises again

not like a white disc to be taken daily,
          a cure-all that will dissolve
pain or grief, but simply as itself,

          as the one eye
of a peacock feather. No trompe l'oeil of metaphor will do
          for what the sun does,

filling in the world's colors, bringing it back to us,
          common and miraculous.
Here comes the orange garbage truck with its long

          automated arm
and claw to grab our standard-size, dull green containers
          and empty them into

the compactor. One two-ply plastic sack splits open,
               a piñata that spills
a cascade of newspapers, chicken bones, disposable diapers,

               mussel shells, and the confetti
of vegetable peelings into the gutter. Let the garbage stink a
        thousand flagrantly
               fragrant ways. I want the day

as is and not as if. Flocks of grackles are migrating, purple-black
        whirlwind
               of thrumming wings that settle
for a moment in the pin oak so that the bare tree sings,

               gossips, and complains, a hundred
rusty hinges, and then stands speechless after its black foliage rises
               and flies north.

My older daughter wakes, runs into the living room,
               and calls me "dummo"
for scribbling shadows in my notebook on such a sun-winged

               morning. To prove me wrong
she goes outside barefoot in her nightgown, as is, and writes
               with one small finger

her own name *Eleanor, Eleanor* ("vee-ur, vee-ur")
               over and over, up and down
the street, on car windshields turned golden-green with pine pollen.

LINDA PASTAN

Wherever We Travel

Wherever we travel
it seems to take the same
few hours to get there.

The plane rises over clouds
into an unmarked sky,
comes down through clouds

to what we have to believe
is a different place. But here
are the same green road signs

the numbered highways
of home, with cars going
back and forth to houses

with chimneys and windows
identical to the ones we thought
we had left behind.

The radio blares familiar
radio music. Soon we will knock
on a door and someone will greet us,

will pull us into a room
we have never seen
but already know by heart.

Near the Sacrificial Site

Paestum, 1997

On an afternoon like this
I want permission to forget
the many varieties of cruelty.
I want the only figures of the past to be
ancestors of these wild
poppies, of this chestnut tree
whose blossoms break through
the hardest wood. I know that cruelty
flourishes just down the road, persistent
as these gnarled roots which overrun
the partly ruined woods.
But on an afternoon like this—
Old Master clouds and waterfalls of light—
I ask for the mercies of amnesia.
I want to open myself to the sun
which I know has killed
with its munificence,
to smell the foxglove
with no thought of the poison
hidden in its leaf.

SUZANNE PAOLA

Pentecost

Cracked Sunday. Babble
of backyard voices,
witnessing over barbecue & open flame.

Gulls cry
above the peeling, fish-slicked decks of trawlers
as if they have something to say besides hunger.

I tell you these things, O Theophilus—

so you will know the apostles when they come
swollen-throated on the esplanade's karaoke stand
singing *Volare, volare*

there, where the Georgia-Pacific plant
belches clouds at the clouds,
mimicking the sky, answering it—

Then motion, an air, a wind—

Why do you stand gazing up to heaven?

VALERIE MARTIN

The Change

Gina had all the symptoms: sleep disturbances, hot flashes, irritability, weight gain, loss of libido, aching joints, and heart palpitations. The one she complained of most was hot flashes, which she dealt with by throwing off her clothes and cursing. As far as Evan was concerned, her irritability was the worst symptom; she was increasingly difficult to get along with. Churlish, he told her. Her lack of interest in sex was possibly more frustrating, though he admitted to himself that he found her less desirable because she was so uncivil, so he did not suffer unduly from wanting her and being rejected. When they did make love, it was a wrestling match, which Evan enjoyed well enough. They had never been much for tender embraces.

Her work was changing, too; it was getting darker. As he stood looking at an engraving of trees, of a dark forest, he wondered how it could all seem so clear when it was almost entirely black. She was working all the time, well into the nights, because she couldn't sleep. Often enough he found her in the mornings curled up under a lap rug on the cot in her cluttered, inky little studio with the windows open and the chill early morning light pouring in.

She wasn't taking care of herself properly, not eating enough, not washing enough, she hardly took any exercise at all. Sometimes she lay around the living room all day, napping or reading magazines, getting up now and then to rummage around in her studio, then back to the couch, where she left ink stains on the upholstery. There were dustballs under the beds and in the corners of the rooms, dishes always stacked in the sink.

"It's driving me crazy," Evan complained. "Can't we get someone in to clean this place, since you can't keep up with it?"

She gave him a cold, reproachful glare over her magazine. "I *can* keep up with it," she said. "I just *don't* keep up with it."

"Well, then, hire someone who will."

"You hire someone," she replied. "Since it bothers you so much."

Evan turned away. He did all the cooking as it was. How could he possibly take on the cleaning as well? And he had no idea how to hire someone. He went to the kitchen and threw open the refrigerator. "And what are we going to eat for dinner?" he shouted to her. "This refrigerator is practically empty."

"We'll go out," she shouted back.

They went out. She was in a good mood for a change. They laughed, drank too much wine, walked back through the city streets with their arms locked around each other, made love on the living room floor. Evan went to bed but she wouldn't go with him. She went to her studio, and twice when he woke in the night, he saw that the light was still on.

The next day she was a harridan again, peevish and distracted. His own work was going poorly, he had taken on too much and had two deadlines he didn't think he could make. When he complained to her, she shrugged. "Then don't make them," she said. "Tell the editor you can't do it."

"Right," he said. "And then she never calls on me again. I need the work."

"You always say that," she snapped. "And you always have more work than you can do. So, obviously you don't need it."

Evan followed her out of the room into her studio. "I don't always have more than I can do. Sometimes I don't have any. It's feast or famine in this business, as you well know."

Gina yawned, put her hands on her hips, and stretched, making an agonized face at him. "Jesus, my back hurts," she said.

"It's freezing in here," he said, moving toward the open window. "Why don't you close this?"

But before he could reach it she blocked his path. "Don't close the window," she said angrily.

"Ugh," Evan said. "What is that?" For on the windowsill were the remains of some animal. Evan pushed past his wife to get a closer look. It was the back half of a mouse, tail, feet, gory innards.

"Where did this come from?" he said.

"The cat must have left it." She turned away, bending over a partially engraved plate.

"We don't have a cat."

All at once she was angry, as if he'd done something annoying.

"The neighbor's cat," she sputtered. "Would you just leave it. I'll take care of it."

"It's disgusting," he said. He looked around the room at the half-empty coffee cups, the dishes with crumbs and bits of old sandwiches or dried cottage cheese stuck to them, the confusion of ink and paper, copper plates, presses, the disorder of the bottles of acids and resins, the writing desk overflowing with unanswered mail, bills, and photographs. "This whole room is disgusting," he concluded. "How can you find anything in here?"

To which she replied, "Who asked you to come in here? Will you get out of here?" And she pushed him out the door.

They were invited to a dinner party. Gina was in her studio until it was almost time to leave. Then she came out, washed her hands, combed her hair, threw on a skirt, and said she was ready. Evan had showered, shaved, dressed carefully, even polished his shoes. He looked at her skeptically. "That's it?" he said. "You're ready?"

"Why not?" she said.

No jewelry, he thought. No makeup, no perfume. There had been a time when it took her at least an hour to dress for a party.

The party went well, it was easy conversation, good wine, old friends, until a couple Gina and Evan had not seen for some time arrived. Evan spotted the woman, Vicky, first, smiled and waved as he caught her eye. Something was different about her, he thought, but he couldn't be sure. She looked great, very bright, very intense. Her blouse had flecks of gold in it; she was sparkling. Gina, standing next to him, laughing at something their host was saying, turned and saw the woman, too. "Oh my God," she said softly. Vicky moved slowly toward them, smiling.

Seeing Gina's drop-jawed amazement, the host said confidentially, "She's been done." Evan sent him an inquiring look, to which he responded by tapping his lower jaw with the backs of his fingers.

Vicky had stopped to speak to someone else. Evan watched her, though he tried not to stare. In a distant, agreeable way he had always admired her. The last time he had seen her, several months ago, he had observed that her delicate beauty was fading. Now she looked good, he thought. She'd changed her hair, too, probably to disguise the more surprising change in her face. They'd done a good job on her. Perhaps her mouth was a little stretched at the corners, and of course the flesh around her chin looked tight. She broke away from her conversation and continued toward Gina and Evan.

"Vicky, how are you?" Evan said, catching her outstretched hand in his own, as if he were retrieving her, he thought, or pulling her out of a fish tank. "It's good to see you."

He was aware of Gina at his side, of her steady, even breathing, but he didn't see her face until it was too late. "Have you lost your mind?" she said sharply to Vicky. "Why would you do something like that? You look awful."

Vicky missed a beat to astonishment and another to dismay, but that was all. "I may have lost my mind," she said, "but you seem to have lost your manners."

Evan turned on his wife. He was so angry he wanted to slap her. "For God's sake, Gina," he said. "Are you drunk?"

Gina blinked her eyes rapidly, ignoring him. She was concentrated on Vicky, who was easing herself away. "So you count on people not to say anything. Do you tell yourself they don't notice?"

"Excuse me," Vicky said, disappearing into the crowd.

"It's ridiculous," Gina continued. "She looked perfectly fine before. Now she looks like something from television, like a talk show host."

"I think we'd better go," Evan said, trying to take her arm, but she shook him off.

"Will you calm down," she said.

So they stayed and the rest of the evening passed uneventfully, but Evan was miserable and felt humiliated. At dinner they were seated as far from Vicky and her husband as possible, probably at her request, Evan thought. Vicky was the center of attention; Evan could hear her tinkling laugh, but couldn't bring himself to look her way. Gina leaned out past him now and then to shoot a disapproving look toward the offending jawline, but she said nothing more about it, and once she got into a conversation with her neighbor, which Evan joined, she seemed to forget the unpleasant incident. They talked about publishing, the neighbor was also a journalist, and then about travel. Gina told a funny story about a hotel they had stayed in on a Greek island, and Evan, though he had heard this story before, though he had actually been there when the porter threw Gina's suitcase out the window, found himself laughing as heartily as their friend. He applied himself to his wine and resolved to forgive his wife.

Evan noticed the book a few times before he actually picked it up to look at it. He'd seen it on the table in the living room, half buried in a pile of magazines, and on the kitchen table, and once on the nightstand next to their bed. A woman's book about women, he thought, about all the trials of their biology and psychology, the special wonderfulness of it all and the failure of men to comprehend any of it, though it was going on right under their noses. Women lapped this stuff up like cream, even intelligent women like Gina, which was what really made it annoying. Here was the book again, jammed between the cushions of the couch with a pencil stuck in it to mark the page. He pulled it out and opened it to the page with the pencil. The chapter was titled "No Longer a Woman," and it told all about the biological changes attendant on the menopause, the shrinking of the uterus, the drying out of vaginal tissue, the atrophy of the ovaries, the steady depletion of estrogen. Pretty dry reading, Evan thought with a sardonic chuckle. He put the book back where he had found it and wandered off to his desk, where his article was not taking shape. No longer a woman, he thought. But if not a woman, then what? It was ridiculous. When was a woman ever not a woman? All the symptoms Gina complained of only proved she was a woman, and a susceptible one at that, which was part of being a woman, too. An old woman was still a woman, still behaved as she always had, only more so. Evan thought of his grandmother. Not an old woman but an old lady. She wore violet perfume, he could still remember it, and was fond of a certain candy, a puffy, spongy, fruit-flavored ball that came in tins; he hadn't seen any in years. She was small, bent, arthritic, but industrious to the end. She did a little gardening on the last day of her life. She had survived her husband by twenty years. Perfectly nice, perfectly sexless. Serene, agreeable. Everyone loved her.

Though he remembered that once, when he was praising this wonderful woman to his mother, she had commented drily, "Yes, she's very nice now. But she wasn't always."

* * *

Their son, Edward, called. Gina answered the phone. Evan stood by waiting for his turn; he was fond of his son and looked forward to these weekly calls. Gina was smiling. She laughed at some witticism and said, "Watch out for that." Then for several minutes she fell silent. Her eyes wandered around the room, never settling, and she shifted her weight from foot to foot restlessly. At last she said, distantly, "That's really great, dear. Here's your father. I'll talk to you next week," and held out the phone to Evan.

While he stood talking to Edward, Gina sat down at the table and pulled off her sweater. Then, as Edward went on about his psychology class, she stripped off her shirt and bra. She stretched her arms out across the table and rested her head upon them. Evan turned away from her and tried to concentrate on his son's description of his daily life. When he hung up the phone she was sitting up, blotting her forehead with her sweater.

"You were a little abrupt with him," Evan said. "He asked if you were okay."

"Of course I'm okay," she said.

Evan took a seat next to her and watched as she pulled her shirt back over her head. "Did he tell you about his psychology professor?"

"Yes," she said. "He talks too much."

Evan ran his hand through his thinning hair, trying to stroke down his impatience. "You're not the only one who's getting older, you know."

She pushed back her chair, dismissing him. She was on her way to her studio. "It's not the same," she said in parting. "It's different."

It was always different, he thought. They wanted to be treated the same, but only with the understanding that they deserved special treatment because they were different. It was true that they had been treated as if they were different for a long time, but they had been treated as different in the wrong way, they were not different in that way. What was different was the deal they got, the way they were treated, which was never fair. He loosened his collar; his face felt hot. But oh no, it wasn't anything that wasn't his fault. It wasn't hormones surging uncontrollably like guerilla fighters, it was just his lousy blood pressure which was elevated by his annoyance with his wife's suffering, and if he was uncomfortable, if he felt a little snappish, well, it was all his fault, because *her* bad temper was a symptom, and *his* was just plain old garden-variety bad temper, typical in the male. He got up and staggered into his study, where his article accosted him, demanding what he could not, because of Gina, seem to give it: his undivided attention. He turned away and went into the kitchen to make coffee.

Gina had gone out to have lunch with a friend. Evan was alone in the apartment with his article. He sat at his desk reading over his notes, listening to the taped interview he had done with a teenaged girl who, he recalled, had been dressed in something that resembled two pieces of bicycle tubing. It depressed him to listen to her agitated, rage-filled monologue. She had a vocabulary of twenty-five words or so, insufficient to express any but the most basic threats and complaints. She was the current girlfriend of a gang member named Smak; Evan's article was about these girls, the attendants of brutal young men, about their precarious, angry, voluptuous, and mindless daily lives. On the tape she was trying to explain to Evan that she did not get up at the same time every day, which was why school was not a possibility for her.

He switched off the tape machine and stared at his bright computer screen for several minutes, but nothing came to him so he switched that off, too. Then he got up and wandered through the apartment to Gina's studio.

The lunch was a kind of celebration; she'd finished all the work scheduled for a show next month. There were two new engravings on the drying rack, the rest were stacked away in two big portfolios, ready to go. As Evan stood looking at one on the rack, a line from one of her catalogues ran through his head: "She is a woman who has never stopped loving the forest." They had a joke about it, a follow-up line: "And she is a woman who has never stopped living in Brooklyn."

For twenty years her subject had been the same, but this didn't mean her work had not changed. In Evan's opinion the change had been gradual and persistent. She was more patient, saw more clearly, though the prints were progressively darker. That was the odd, wonderful thing about the newer prints; though they seemed to be covered with ink they were full of an odd kind of light, an almost subterranean glow. In this one, for instance, he could see through a tangle of vegetation to the ground beneath, and on that dark ground he could make out the tracks of some small animal, a mouse or a chipmunk. In both the prints on the rack, the viewpoint was high, as if the viewer were above it all, in a tree perhaps, looking down. Evan studied the second one. He seemed to be falling into it; it was truly an exhilarating angle. There, as he looked deeper and deeper through the accumulation of lines, he made out something extraordinary. He crouched down, close to the paper. It was the small hind foot of a rabbit, no bigger than his fingernail, but perfectly clear. In the next second, he knew, it would be gone.

He went to the portfolio, opened it, looked at the first print. Again the odd feeling of vertigo seized him as he looked down upon the teeming world of branches and vines. He could almost hear the dull buzz of insect life, breathe the oxygen-laden air. "These are terrific," he said aloud. No wonder she had been so absorbed, so distracted, so uninterested in the daily course of her life. He felt a little stab of jealousy. His own work did not claim him; he had to drag himself to it. But that feeling passed quickly. He sat down on her cot, flushing with excitement, imagining how the room would look filled with his wife's strange vision. He heard her key in the door, her footsteps in the hall, then she was standing in the doorway looking in at him.

"What are you doing in here?" she said, just an edge of territorial challenge in her tone.

"I was looking at the new work," he said.

She leaned against the doorframe, pushed her hair off her forehead. She'd had a few drinks at lunch, celebrating. "Well, what do you think?" she said.

"I think it's just amazing," he said. "It's so good I had to sit down here and mull it over."

She sagged a little more in the doorway, smiling now but anxious. "Do you really think so? I've been almost afraid for you to see it."

"Oh, my dear," he said.

Tears filled her eyes. She brushed them away with the back of one hand. "I'm so happy," she said. She came into the room and sat beside him, still wiping away tears. "These stupid tears," she said impatiently.

Evan put his arm around her, muttered into her shoulder, "I'm so proud of you." There they sat for some time, contented, holding on to one another as if they were actually in the forest of her dreams.

There was always a letdown after she'd finished a block of work, Evan told himself in the difficult days that followed. She was petulant and weepy, angry with the gallery owner, who had been her friend and supporter for years, complaining about every detail of the installation. She hardly slept at night, though what she did in her studio Evan couldn't figure out. She wasn't working and she hadn't, as she usually did between showings, cleaned the place up. But night after night he woke just long enough to watch her get up, pull on her robe, and go out, then he saw the light from her studio. During the day she lay about the apartment, napping or reading, getting nothing done and snapping at him if he so much as suggested a trip to the grocery. He tried to ignore her, spent his days struggling with his article, which resisted his efforts so stubbornly he sometimes sat at his desk for hours, literally pulling at what he called the remains of his hair. Finally he began to have trouble sleeping, too. He lay on his back in the darkness while panic gripped his heart, unable to move or to rest. When he did sleep, he had strange, unsettling dreams in which he was lost, pursued by something terrifying, powerful, something silent and brooding, something with wings.

One night, waking in terror from such a dream, he found himself, as he often did, alone in the bed. Once his heart slowed down and strength returned to his legs, he resolved to get up. His throat was parched, he felt dehydrated, as if he had been wandering in a desert. Pursued by what? he thought as he sat up and fumbled around for his slippers. Some desert creature? A creature with claws and wings and the face of a woman who would pose some unanswerable riddle before tearing him to bits? The idea amused him as he stumbled to the kitchen and switched on the lights, which made him recoil so violently he switched them back off. He poured himself a glass of water, and stood, still sleep-shocked, gazing out the kitchen window at the back of the building across the alley. Above it he could see the milky luminescence of the half-moon. He finished his water, feeling quiet now, and friendly.

The light from Gina's studio made a pool across the kitchen floor. He put his glass in the sink and followed this light to her room. The double doors had glass insets, but the glass was mottled so as not to be transparent. They were closed, but not tightly—in fact one stood free of the latch and could be opened noiselessly with a push. He didn't want to startle her, but if she was asleep he didn't want to wake her, either. "Gina?" he said softly once, then again. Carefully he pushed the door open a few inches. He could see the cot from where he was; she wasn't in it. He opened the door a little farther, then all the way. The window stood open, the room was bright and cold; Gina was not in it.

It took him a moment to apprehend this information. He looked around anxiously, as if he could make her materialize by his determination to find her there. He went to the living room, perhaps she was sleeping on the couch; he looked in the bathroom and then the bedroom, though, of course, he knew she was not there. He glanced at the clock, three a.m. He went back to the studio.

What did it mean? How often in the past months, when he had believed her to be here in this room had she been . . . wherever she was? His heart ached in his chest, he laid his hand upon it. She had a lover, there could be no doubt of it. That was why she was so tired all the time, why she slept all day, and why she was so cold and bitter.

Evan switched off the light and went to sit on the couch in the living room in the dark. He would wait for her; they would have it out. His rival was probably much younger than he was. When women Gina's age could, they often did. He thought of Colette and George Eliot. He would be a young man impressed by her because she was an artist and he was, surely, a nothing, a boy in need of a mother. It went like that; there were countless such stories. The minutes ticked by. He waited in a fog of anxiety and weariness. He wasn't up to the scene to come. Perhaps he should get back in bed and pretend he didn't know. Maybe then the affair would run its course, she would tire of the young man, or he of her, and things would get back to normal.

He was awakened by a clatter coming from Gina's studio. It sounded like someone was smashing china. He leaped to his feet, crossed the narrow hall, and threw open the doors. The early morning light was soft and pale, bathing the scene before him in a wash of pink and gray. Gina was on her hands and knees on the floor just inside the window. Next to her was a broken plate. A few crusts had flown from it and landed near her foot. One was lodged in the cuff of her pants.

"What on earth are you doing?" he cried.

She sat up, rubbing her ankle, picking out the bit of bread. "What does it look like I'm doing?" she said crossly. "I'm trying to get up off the floor."

"But where have you been? You weren't here."

She lifted her head toward the window. "I was on the fire escape."

She couldn't have come in the door, Evan reasoned. She would have had to walk through the living room and he would have seen her. "What were you doing out there?" he complained. "Didn't you hear me call you?"

"No," she said. "I guess I fell asleep." She got to her feet, brushing herself off. Evan pushed past her and stuck his head out the window. "How could you sleep out here?" he called back to her. In the summer she kept plants on the landing, herbs and geraniums, and on hot nights she sometimes took a cushion and sat among the pots. But now there was nothing but the cold metal, the cold air, and the cold stars fading overhead in a pale sky. The stairs led down to a narrow alleyway, which opened into a school parking lot that was fenced and locked at night. She couldn't have gone down there. His eye was caught by something on the landing below. It was a long brown feather with a black bar across it. He turned from the window to his wife, who was sitting on the cot, her head in her hands.

"You don't expect me to believe that," he said.

She raised her head and gave him a brief weary inspection, as if she were looking at an annoying insect. "I don't care what you believe," she said.

"Gina, what's happening to you?" he exclaimed. "You disappear in the middle of the night, you tell me an absurd lie nobody would believe, and then you give me your too-tired-to-care routine."

"I'm not tired," she said. "I just don't care."

"We can't go on like this," he said, in despair.

"I know it," she said.

*　*　*

But they did go on. What else, Evan thought, could they do? He accepted her story, partly because he couldn't come up with an alternative scenario—she had been coming in through the window, and the fire escape, as she pointed out, led nowhere—and partly because it didn't seem to matter. He didn't think she was having an affair because she didn't act like someone who was in love; she was neither defensive nor elated, and she seemed completely uninterested in her own body. What he had often thought of as a brooding sensuality now became just brooding. He continued his struggle with his article, Gina battled it out with her gallery, and finally they were both finished and both were moderately successful. They had a little time to rest, to cast about for new projects. Usually when this happened they gave themselves over to the pleasure of having no deadlines, sleeping late, eating at odd hours, gorging on videos, food, and sex. But this time it was different. Gina was still sleeping very little at night, and she seemed so uninterested in sex Evan made a resolution that he would not initiate it. In the past, he thought gloomily, he had never paid much attention to who started it. Now he was self-consciously aware that it was always him. She rejected him without speaking, with a shrug, or by walking away. And if she did accept his overtures, she hurried him along, as if she didn't really have the time and her mind was somewhere else. He grew sick of trying and sick of waiting. Winter was dragging on; the weather was rotten, cold and rainy.

Evan was drinking too much, and for the first time in his life he began to put on weight. One Sunday when the sun was shining for a change and there was a hint of warmth in the air, he ran into a neighbor at the farmers' market. During their conversation Evan jokingly mentioned the latter problem; the drinking was a secret he was keeping even from himself.

"It happens to the best of us," his neighbor said. "Especially at our age. I've joined a gym; it's not far from here. It's made a big difference in how I feel."

Evan had to admit that his neighbor looked fit and energetic. "Give me a call," the neighbor concluded. "I go two or three times a week. I'll take you over and show you around. Bring Gina, if she's interested."

But of course she wasn't interested. "It's ridiculous," she said, throwing one magazine on the floor and taking up another. "I'm not going to spend my time running on a treadmill like a laboratory rat."

So Evan went alone. He met his friend at the reception desk and received a pass, then a tour of the facility. He was impressed with the size of the place, the up-to-date equipment, swimming pool, racquetball courts—he hadn't played in years but he remembered enjoying the game—there was even a juice and salad bar. It was in this bar, as he was leaving, that he found Vicky and her husband, who waved him over to their table with soft cries of enthusiasm and surprise. As he walked to join them, Evan experienced a mild pang of discomfort; he hadn't seen either of them since Gina had behaved so rudely at the party. But Vicky seemed not to remember, or not to care. Her hand pressed his warmly in greeting and she patted the chair next her, inviting him to sit.

"So you're thinking of joining up?" her husband, Victor, inquired.

Evan smiled at him and nodded, looking around the pleasant, busy room. He was thinking, as he always did when he saw them together, Vicky and Victor, such silly names. "It's much bigger than I thought it would be," he said.

Vicky drained her carrot juice. "We've been coming for a year now. It's a lifesaver."

"You look great," Evan said. She really did. She was wearing a sleeveless scoop-neck leotard and leggings so he could see exactly how good she looked. There was just a hint of cleavage visible at the neckline, enough to show that her breasts were still firm, not sallow-looking or wrinkled. Her arms looked firm and strong, too, though the thick cords and darkened skin on the backs of her hands gave some hint of her age. She had a scarf tied around her waist, not the best idea, Evan thought, because it called attention to the small but distinctly round belly just below. He couldn't see her hips. She pushed her hair back from her face, giving Evan a quick, complex look made up in parts of gratitude, flirtation, and suspicion. "Thanks," she said. "I feel great."

Victor patted her shoulder proprietarily. "She's fantastic," he said. Vicky laughed, childishly pleased to be the object of her husband's praise. Evan looked down at himself with fake dismay. "I'll need a lot of work," he said. "It may be too late for me."

"Never too late," Victor assured him. "You're as young as you feel."

Evan wished they could talk about something else, but there was no way to change the subject. This was a gym, after all. The subject was bodies. Victor told Evan about his routine. He liked the stair-step machine, Vicky preferred the treadmill. The aerobic classes were excellent. Vicky even did yoga. The free-weights room was sometimes a little crowded; the young jocks did not always leave the racks in perfect order, that was the only drawback. At last there was a lull long enough for Evan to make an excuse. He had to get back to work, he said. As always, he had a deadline.

"Time for us to hit the showers," Victor said, getting up. He popped Vicky playfully across the shoulders with his towel. "Great to see you," he said, grasping Evan's hand. "Give Gina our best."

Evan noted the brief flash of distress that crossed Vicky's face at the mention of his wife. She remembers perfectly well, he thought. She's just being nice about it. Then he was angry at Gina all over again. What right had she to criticize this nice woman because she cared enough about her appearance to have her face lifted? What was wrong with staying fit and wanting to look good for each other, as Vicky and Victor obviously did?

Evan left the gym with a printed sheet of membership privileges and prices gripped tightly in his hand. Filled with resolution and optimism, he stopped in the chilly parking lot to look it over. This was a good thing to do, he told himself. He wanted to be like Vicky and Victor. Gina would ridicule him but he didn't care. He wanted to feel good about himself, he wanted to change his life. Carefully he folded his informational paper and put it deep in his coat pocket.

That night Gina was particularly restless and distracted. Evan made pasta and a salad for dinner but she hardly touched it. She complained that her neck and shoulders were stiff, shrugging repeatedly, trying to loosen up the muscles. Evan told her about the gym, expecting a tirade, or simply a dismissive remark, but to his surprise she listened attentively. In fact, as he explained why he thought it would be a good investment for him, how he feared that his sedentary ways resulted in fatigue and depression, she seemed to focus on him with a distant but sincere interest. "It can't be good for you to be closed up in here with me all the time," she said.

"It's not that," he protested.

She said nothing. Evan chewed a piece of lettuce. He could feel her eyes on his face. At last he looked up at her, expecting to find contempt, or anger, or indifference, but she was studying him with a look of complete sympathy, devoid of pity or self-interest, as if, he thought, she were looking right into his soul and finding it blameless, but also infinitely sad. He felt a hot flush rising to his cheeks and he looked away, at his fork resting among the salad greens, at his half-full glass of wine.

"I think it's a good idea," she said.

They sat together on the couch watching a video. It was a complicated story of intrigue on a Greek island. Evan had chosen it because the cover showed a man standing in front of a white building set against a sky so blue and so clearly warm he wished he was in the picture. The scenery in the film was terrific; the television screen seemed to pour warmth and color into their drab living room. When it was over Evan talked a little about how much he wanted to travel, to go to Greece again, and also to Italy and Spain, warm sunny countries where the people were relaxed and friendly and the food was fresh, healthful, and prepared with care and enthusiasm. Now that their son was grown they could think about going off-season, when there were no tourists. Gina listened, inserting qualifiers here and there—the food in Spain was notoriously filthy, the Italians were far from relaxed—but she seemed more amused than irritated by his aimless fantasies. "You're full of desires today," she said.

"It's true," he admitted. "I am." He rubbed his hand along her thigh, nuzzled his face against her shoulder. She neither responded nor pushed him away. He brought his hand up to her breast, took her earlobe gently between his teeth. "Please don't," she said softly.

He dropped back on the couch, letting out a sigh of frustration.

"I'm sorry," she said, getting up.

"Don't worry about it," he said.

She went into her studio and began gathering up dishes,

wadding up pieces of paper. She left the doors open and Evan could see her from where he sat. She went into the kitchen carrying plates, came back with a garbage bag. Evan looked at the clock; it was after midnight. A great time for a little light cleaning, he thought. "A little night cleaning," he called to her.

"I can't stand it anymore," she said, amiably.

"Me neither," Evan said, but softly, to himself. She didn't hear it. After a few minutes he realized he was falling asleep. He got up, pulling off his clothes as he went to bed.

The dream ended, as he had known it must, with his missing the plane. Evan woke feeling breathless. He had been running, but they kept the planes across a busy six-lane highway from the check-in. There was a fence, too, he recalled, chain-link, tall, over six feet. He rolled onto his side and looked at the clock. It was five a.m. Gina had still not come to bed. He sat up, rubbing his head, disoriented and strangely apprehensive. After a few moments he got up and made his way to the kitchen. While he stood at the sink drinking water, it dawned on him that the lights in Gina's studio were off. She must have decided to sleep in there. Usually when he found her asleep, the lights were on, the book she had been reading had slipped to the floor or lay, still open, beneath her hand. He stepped out into the hall.

The day was just beginning to dawn and there was enough gray light for him to see his way. It was, he thought, the most beautiful time of day. The air was still, the building all around him wrapped in a nearly palpable silence, yet alive with the impending and inevitable intensification of light. It was warm in the hall; the apartment was overheated and there was no way to adjust it. A blast of cool air greeted him as he reached Gina's studio. There he stood absorbing one shock after the other.

She had left both the doors and windows wide open. The room was in perfect order, down to the pencils. Some of the habitual clutter had even been stored away in boxes, which were stacked against one wall. The cot was made up neatly: Gina was not in it. Nor was she anywhere else in the room. He said her name once, turned and looked out into the living room, but of course she wasn't there, either. He crossed the orderly studio—it seemed alien yet familiar to him, like a room in a dream—to look out on the fire escape, which he found, as he expected, unoccupied. Why was this happening? he thought. Why couldn't everything just go on as it always had? He gazed up at the pale sky, down at the iron clutter of the fire escape, across the narrow ugly yard at the opposite building. He felt an ineffable sadness curling up into his consciousness like a twining plume of smoke. The building was mostly dark, no one was up yet. One narrow window had a light on, probably a bathroom light left on all night.

He had the uncanny feeling that he was being watched. An abrupt snapping sound drew his eyes up to the ledge at the top, just one story above his own.

That was when he saw the owl.

His sadness was dissipated by this wondrous sight. He leaned out the window, craning his neck to see more clearly. "Wow," he said. "An owl in Brooklyn."

A big owl, too, or so it seemed to him. He reflected that he had never actually seen an owl before, at least not at such close range. The bird was perfectly still but its head was inclined forward, its golden eyes were focused on Evan. Then, to his astonishment, with a sudden convulsion of motion that was as soundless as it was alarming, the owl opened its wings and flew directly at him. The distance between them, some thirty yards, disappeared in a second. Evan reeled away from the window, aware only of fierce talons extended in his direction. In the next moment he stood clutching the edge of Gina's drawing table, and the owl was perched comfortably on the window ledge, not ten feet away.

His momentary terror faded, replaced by fascination and wonder. The bird was evidently not going to attack him. There was a raised metal bar along the sill, part of the fire escape, and the owl had wrapped its feet around this. He could see the talons sticking out beneath the thick brown fluff of the legs, black and long and sharp as a cat's claws. The bill, too, looked sharp and dangerous, like a hard black finger pointing down between the large golden eyes. These eyes were fixed on Evan's face with unblinking, unnerving directness. They seemed to be looking right through him, possibly at something behind him. He shifted uneasily from one foot to the other. "I'd ask you to stay," he said, "but we're fresh out of mice."

The bird opened its beak, as if to speak, then spun its head around to face the courtyard, where some tiny motion or sound, invisible or inaudible to Evan, attracted its attention. The whole maneuver was so sudden he had only an impression of having seen it, but it seemed to him the bird's head went all the way around. The eyes drilled through him again. What a disturbing thing it was to be scrutinized in this way by a creature who had, he knew, no sympathy with him. Again the owl opened its beak, but this time a sound issued forth, a high-pitched, startling scream, such as a frightened woman might make. It was so loud and sudden it made Evan step back. Then, as suddenly, the bird was silent again. "Please," Evan said. "You'll wake the neighbors." The owl, unconcerned, fell to picking at its chest feathers. Evan stepped closer, quietly, stealthily, as if the bird didn't know with each second exactly where he was. He was so close he could have reached out to touch the beautiful mottled wings, though he knew he would not dare. The owl raised its strange, otherworldly face, made a calm sidestep on the bar, dipped its head, then refocused on his face.

"Why have you come here?" Evan asked.

But the owl only stared at him and he felt foolish for speaking. With the intrusion of this portentous creature, all the tedium and anxiety of his life had fallen away. A thrill, as of discovery, passed through him, but he did not move. It was best to be still in such a presence, which surely would not stay long or ever come again.

Thunder, Perfect Mind

She would stand in that place
where pilgrims and petitioners
who craved God waited for
her answers. Intermediary,

she would pace as if chained
to it: the division in mind.
She was no go-between,
finally. Look at it, she was

Sophia or Ruah, she was
hokhmah. Her shopping cart
full of bird masks, low-watt light-
bulbs, overturned in the aisle.

I know her, you know her.
I knelt to help her. Nagging
voice over the intercom:
Let's buy a hundred useless things!

Let's get out of here, Wing,
I said. But there are so many
precipices when you are
following her. And little meaning.

She roared at the angels
crowding in. I don't like them much,
they snore too loud, she said.
She won't wait for you to agree

or disagree. It's quite
clearly her world, her residence.
Her hair is blue, yes, blue.
Not the blue of an animal

sacrifice, the other
hue. Storm, invisible foundation.

JOSEPH MILLAR

Outside Monterey

Outside Monterey the highway
runs by the sea and the torch singer
on the radio has a voice like twilight:
"I couldn't love you more, child,
if time was running out..."

My ten-year-old shaved his head when his mother left,
looked oddly more adult last night,
coloring the Stay Out sign for his bedroom door.
Earlier I stopped to buy goldfish, dinner
for the snake he keeps
trapped with its hunger
in a glass box.

Night drifts into the artichoke fields
and the swallows veer off toward the hills,
bent wings scissoring the dusk.
I park under a tree, lean back
with the lights off and the engine running.

I want to travel all night like this, the ocean
whispering beside me in the darkness,
passing no one on the road.

Auspicious Things

In a dream: a poem from the next century.
—Elias Canetti

Of the thirty-eight things listed, most are slight,
would hardly register otherwise: an albino

sifting through trash in an alley; cracks
forming & widening between lakes of snow

on a windshield; the foil from chewing gum.
In the time of the thirteenth *baktun,*

says another source, the copper anklet-
charm of the sun will darken & smoke

red, like the thighs of this dancer,
oiled, with *coquillas* & beads, who kneels

& lets the fire from the sweetgrass burn him
high on each leg. In his face & hands,

raveled & barely comprehensible,
are calendar-glyphs: jaguars and a zero.

Two thousand twelve A.D. Take it or leave it.
Late winter light on bricks, a taste of perfume.

Meditation

The world sneaks back. Like the small dog that lives up the street,
small enough he needn't wait for her to open the gate.

Alone, she goes farther inside where the shore's swept
so clean it becomes meaningless.

And that's the beauty of it, looking down the beach
it's empty, a long well of sunlight and heat,

until she hears the terrier's unclipped nails
and the rain and wind pick up—tiny bits of sea glass.

No, she says, her own dog hearing too, *he stinks.*
All right, she says, getting up to let the other dog in.

Snow

Each flake is an old Cape Cod church
with its steeple broken off.

Still it is possible
to locate a hymn within.

I was handed a thin
porcelain implement by a man

prepared to die.
He said, They are alike:

the baton of the maestro,
the whitestick of the sightless.

Chapel

Laundry strung between high windows, bilious
in breezy light. A circle of uniformed boys

in a courtyard kicking a soccer ball, and someone
upstairs practicing piano. In the dream

a ceramic creamer painted with wild sunflowers.
Streaks of rainbow plumage from small boats

going away. Motor oil. Olive oil. Angels that leap
from the mind onto the chapel ceiling, a man supine

in midair—this is renovation. Now we must wait
for the fish light to surface: a mackerel or a perch.

Rust-colored sausages in a butcher shop dangling
like wind chimes. When I woke the actual creamer

was bursting with purple grapes, the soccer ball beneath
the staircase, unnoticed, like the world. We say

we have come to see memory's bright scales, though
the early fog has swallowed canals and the sea.

It's barely dawn. We should sleep. Somewhere a painter
dips her brush, adding pale blue to the wings.

Haydn, 1772

Haydn conducting the first performance
of the *Farewell Symphony* for Count Esterhazy
in his palace, the work composed so that
here and there an instrument would cease,
each bewigged and bespectacled musician
pack up his case and depart, the rich sounds
in that great hall, with its plaster curlicues
and cherubs and six-foot candelabra, diminishing
like candles going out one by one in a chandelier,
until the last musician, the composer himself,
closed the door behind him. That moment
when the door closes, leaving the count,
second only to the Emperor in property and power,
seated on his red-plush, gilt-edged throne,
his hushed courtiers looking toward him,
his lands tilled and tidy beyond the palace:
—that moment when the count leans forward
and stares at the music stands and empty chairs.

Incident from the Day of the Dead

Miguel told me he had been home alone for two hours, studying. It was in Guanajuato when he was twelve years old, on the Day of the Dead, and his mother and sisters had gone to tidy his father and grandparents' graves.

He didn't remember why he looked from his book on the dining room table to the sideboard in the corner, where his baby sister had surrounded the makeshift altar with the candies his grandmother liked so much and the small dark cigars his father and grandfather were so fond of. It was probably a sound of some sort, he said, a chair creaking maybe. But when he looked, there was his father, turned the other way, holding a cigar under his nose, sideways, like a flute, sniffing the length of it as he did when he was alive.

The old man was so intent on the cigar, his face serious, that he didn't notice Miguel at first. He was sitting on a dining room chair, in the black suit he had been buried in, and was leaning toward the altar, as if he had just picked up the cigar. Then he tensed and a moment later turned toward Miguel, and they sat that way, looking at each other across the table in the late afternoon light. And that's how Miguel knew, he said, that only a table separates the living from the dead.

"What did you do then?" I asked.

Miguel shook his head.

We had been talking for hours about one thing and another, sipping beer at my kitchen table, while the household slept and the night wind buffeted the tiny house on the Northern California coast. Our talk had wandered onto the brushes we had had with the dead, and he had told this story about his father, and now it was clear he had said all he intended to say.

"That's it?" I asked. "Nothing more?"

"No. Nothing."

We sat in silence for several moments. *Just as he and his father had*, I thought, and I said aloud to continue the conversation, "How long did you sit that way?"

He shrugged. "My mother and sisters returned soon after."

"And he was gone then?"

He clenched his jaws and looked past me toward the window.

I knew that if I continued my questioning I would be invading a reserve in him that I had learned to respect, and I must admit that I was too timid or unwilling to hurl myself at the barricade of facial expressions he had thrown up between us, and there the matter ended.

But I also felt that *I* had somehow failed, failed in the same way Miguel and his father had failed with each other.

At the same time, I felt that the incident was not finished. Miguel had told me the story, and somehow the story and the telling and what had just occurred at my kitchen table were now joined in a single event. It made no difference if Miguel and I never spoke of the incident again, or if my insistence had destroyed our friendship, which, I'm relieved to say, it did not.

It was as though the story told me in a California kitchen by a middle-aged man about an incident from his childhood in Mexico now included me, was somehow mine as much as it was his, and continued from that point, having less and less to do with our friendship, or even us. His reticence and my timidity, both our failures, and his failure with his father and his father's failure with him, were what the story was about.

And now, dear reader, just as I became part of the story Miguel told me, so you have become part of the story, too. It is as if we sat across from each other at a kitchen table, although I am no longer here and possibly wrote these words years ago. I may even no longer be alive. You, however, read these words as if I am sitting here with you, and that has allowed me to include you in the tale, a tale whose telling beyond this point I am either unwilling or unable to provide.

Corita's Tank

for James Carroll

The freeway shudders under heavy trailers,
and layers of accumulating afternoon heat.
    A cormorant perches atop an inlet piling,
the creosote log, driven into the silt, swaying
    in a trace of tide. Desolate gravel raked
around the storage farms, the winter-fuel stockpile.
    Then, monumentally squat, the natural gas
tank, its white bulk painted with four rough stripes
    each band of color an act of faith
in an art to alter, however slightly, the public soul.

In November when Vietnamese writers visited
and ate lunch with us under the founders' portraits,
    Mr. Hu'u Thinh said that in Vietnam no one felt
censored. Writing was for the "survival of the nation,"
    a selflessness asked of all, especially artists.
I was polite, but happy to tell him about Sister Corita,
    her profile of Ho Chi Minh on the gas tank,
how on the right side of the red swath you can see
    the curve of his brow, the beard's unmistakable
wisps, one eye gazing westward over this nation
    and surprised to find itself hiding up there,
the smuggled face of the revolution in plain view.

    I am sweating at the wheel, inching forward,
trying not to graze the man in a field jacket as he pushes
    a market basket along the breakdown lane.
I have seen him before, and his redeemable trash,
    the empties, a comforter. Some tap their temples,
call him a fucking nut, but a sadness thick as heat
    off the freeway rises in me when I picture him

falling into fitful, dangerous sleep, or leaning to piss
    on the scored abutments, their peeling red paint.
Maybe it's an allegiance mixed in with the sadness,
    like Williams for those on the Passaic,
reluctant intuition that no matter how desolate
    or bereft we become, still there are signs
of hidden life, weedy but rooted. Barely audible
    in his helpless discourse to no one,
just visible at the tip of his slow, deeply serious
    finger-fuck-you. It is the simple, blurred
desire to break anything, a face, a fist in the wall.
    A spirit mean as asphalt: pungent, pliable,
staining the heart, spread out over the soul, flattened.

    Maybe he's measuring the steel-gray
stretch of bay out to the island where they aerate
    the sludge. Or maybe he is just aiming
at the jet coming in, dropping a mortar shell down
    an imaginary tube, keying on the glint,
the flare under the aluminum wings coming in,
    coming in over the art of Sister Corita,
over Uncle Ho, over the boiling line of the stalled,
    over the mirror-glass towers of wealth
blinking in code, coming to rest here on the rim
    of a broken wheel, the hub of which
        he thinks of as home.

WILLIAM LOGAN

After Easter

The skylight filled with snow, like whitened ash.
Three traders flagged a taxi going south.
Inside the bank, the ATM spat cash.
You put your shivering fingers to its mouth.

Knowing tomorrow the temperature would rise,
Manhattan churned the Easter snow to mud.
I saw the faintest passion in your eyes.
The doctors found new cancer in your blood.

There is a pocket war in Mexico.
Those years when you were dangerous to know—
Where did they come from? Would they never go?
The market made another leap; the Dow Jones soared.
If love remains, what's left of love is snow:
out in the streets, the choking gutters roared.

Bad Jews

There were only a few perfect spots in the world, and Leo Spivak had finally found one of them, right here in Mendocino. He was stretched out just inside the screen door of the brown-shingled beachfront cottage he and his wife, Rachel, had rented for a week—just the two of them, alone in all this peace and quiet. It was as beautiful and peaceful as a postcard. An adorably disheveled burst of nasturtiums framed the screen door and tumbled down across the tiny lawn of shaved English grass to their own private redwood hot tub. Ocean breezes, tangy with salt, washed over Spivak's face, and through the mist he could hear very clearly the wet, hypnotic slap of water as it lapped at pilings across the cove. He'd been looking for this very spot— these flowers, this breeze, these gently lapping waves—all his life. And now here he was. He found himself seriously mulling over the possibility that he'd never move again—that he would lie quite happily in this precise position, right here by the screen door, until he died.

And then the phone rang. Spivak closed his eyes. "Honey?" he moaned. Rachel was snoozing on the couch; the phone was exactly halfway between them, but Spivak wouldn't have wanted to answer the damn thing even if it had been nestled next to his cheek. Their daughter, Elena, sixteen, was at a tennis camp in Wisconsin that they couldn't afford, and she'd called them twice already in the past three days pleading for more spending money. "C'mon," he said, "you get it, okay? If it's Elena asking for another two hundred bucks, I'm liable to say something I'll regret. I'm not kidding. And anyway, I can't move. I'm in the perfect spot."

Rachel caught the phone just after its third ring. She listened a moment, then her face went slack, and she handed the phone to her husband silently, despite his raised eyebrows. "Hello?" he said, and sat down heavily next to her.

"Leo? This is Inez. Your father's friend in Tucson?" Though

she'd lived in Tucson all her life, the intonations in her voice were Hispanic. Spivak had always been proud of the fact that it didn't matter one bit to him that Inez was Hispanic. His father, on the other hand, the bigoted bastard, had always given Inez a hard time about her heritage, joking with her about Mexican farting contests and calling her a wetback to her face.

"Inez, hey, how are you? How's my father?"

"Oh," she said, and then her voice caught. "That's what I'm calling you about. I'm so sorry to have to tell you this news. Your father's dead, Leo. I'm so sorry."

"He's dead?" Spivak's heart leapt, and then, immediately ashamed of itself, it plunged back into the dark cavern of his chest. "He died? Oh, my gosh, no. When?"

"Last night. I don't know when. They didn't call until this morning."

"Who? The nursing home? Tell me—what happened? What did they say?"

"He fell," Inez said. "He slipped and hit his head. I don't know, they didn't tell me too much. They asked me to call you. I told them I didn't want to do it, but they asked again."

"He just hit his head and died?"

"That's what they told me. He's gone, Leo. He's gone." She was crying now, this old woman—her voice sounded thin and silly to him, suddenly soaked with tears, as though she'd stepped off a ledge into deep water.

"How did you find me at this number?" Spivak asked. As soon as he'd said it he realized how inappropriate it was at a time like this—but he couldn't help himself: he was curious.

"Oh, I called your house," Inez told him. "I spoke to your house sitter?"

"Okay, well, I'm glad you called," he said, though that was, of course, a lie. "Sit tight, Inez. I'll handle everything."

"Do you want me to arrange for a funeral announcement? In the newspaper?"

"Oh, gee. Yeah. Good idea—go ahead and do that. Sure. That'd be great."

"What should I say? About your dad, I mean? For the announcement?"

"What should you say?" Spivak asked. "I don't know." His mind was completely blank. "You knew him. Just say whatever you want. You can make something up."

Over Spivak's objections, Rachel came along with him on the drive from Mendocino to San Francisco, then flew with him to Tucson; why, after all, in the name of God, she asked him, would she have wanted to stay in Mendocino by herself? But once they'd arrived in Tucson and had checked into their motel, Spivak announced his firm intention to take care of all the details of his father's personal effects and funeral arrangements by himself. "You didn't even like him," he reminded her. "I didn't like him, either, but he's my father, so I'm obligated."

"I'm your wife—I'm obligated, too."

"Absolutely not. It's out of the question. Stay right here," he told her. "Go swimming—they've got a great pool here. Work on your tan, read a book. I don't want to hear about you doing anything but relaxing. And whatever you do, don't try to get involved in this funeral thing. We're on vacation. We didn't go on vacation because my father was alive, and now that he's dead, that doesn't mean our vacation is over."

"You're not making any sense. Come on. This is your father we're talking about."

"We've waited for this vacation for two years. I'm not going to have it ruined, and that's that. It's not Mendocino, but at least there's a pool and the sun is shining. Okay, so it's a hundred and eight degrees and there's no ocean. But shut your eyes, use your imagination, you're right back in California. Smell that surf. Just work on your tan and practice your backstroke, and let me handle this my way, okay?"

So while Rachel lounged nervously by the pool at the Marriott, daubing sunblock on her shoulders every five minutes, Spivak, his face set in a grim mask, drove to Desert Angels, his father's nursing home. He stood impatiently in the reception lounge, waiting as the woman behind the counter rummaged through a pile of papers. A moment later she thrust a clipboard full of documents at him. "We're all going to miss your father," she said, her voice full of cheery compassion. "He was such a lively, lively guy. You can fill these out over there." She pointed to a nearby couch.

There was no denying it: the place smelled frankly of urine. Near the door, an old woman sat in a wheelchair, her head sunk so low that her whiskered chin nearly rested on her chest. Her eyes were open, but she seemed to be staring at nothing. She was nodding her head slightly and grunting, making a sound that resembled "uh-huh"—like some sort of relentless, monotonal benediction. *Lively,* Spivak said to himself, rolling his eyes as he filled out forms. *Lively compared to what?*

From where he sat, he could see into the dining room: a morbidly obese woman stood at a lectern reading bingo numbers into a microphone, while a few residents of the nursing home sat like zombies in wheelchairs, some of them hooked to oxygen tanks. Attendants stood by, helping the residents keep track of their progress. "Bingo!" a male attendant said in a loud voice. Somewhere down the hall, someone was screaming.

He handed the clipboard back to the receptionist, who said, "Just sign this release form and you can take your father's personal papers." Spivak scribbled his signature, and she handed him a manila envelope, which he immediately ripped open. Inside were his father's honorable discharge from the Army, a copy of his Social Security card, fourteen dollars, and a typed and notarized Last Will and Testament. The will was worthless; his father had scrawled his own name on both of the lines reserved for witnesses' signatures. Spivak stuffed it back into the envelope and shoved the whole thing into the hip pocket of his shorts.

"Before I go," he said, "would there be anyone available who could talk to me for just a moment about my father? You know—just for some sort of closure? I'm kind of curious about his death. To be perfectly honest with you, I'd sort of convinced myself he'd live forever."

"Of course," she said, and bit her lip. "Just have a seat and I'll get your father's nurse."

In a moment a large woman with masculine features appeared and sat next to him. "You're Mr. Spivak's son?" she said. "I'm Mrs. Mitchell. I stopped in to see your father almost every day. He talked about you all the time. Leo this and Leo that. He was very proud."

"Well, thank you. That's very nice to hear."

"You wanted to know about your father's death," Mrs. Mitchell said. Her eyes narrowed. "Your father slipped and hit his head." Mrs. Mitchell coughed into her hand. "He'd had an accident, and the floor was slippery."

"An accident," Spivak echoed, and nodded thoughtfully.

"Yes. This may be painful, Mr. Spivak. He'd—lost control of his bowels." She saw the look on Spivak's face, and quickly added, "That's not at all unusual among our patients. It happens every day. Apparently he was trying to get to the bathroom." She coughed again.

"You mean my father slipped in his own—?"

"Yes. That's right." She looked away for a moment, and knotted a handkerchief in her lap. "A fall like that . . . internal bleeding, cerebral hemorrhage." She shrugged. "Your father hadn't been well, you know. He was frail. He'd fallen a number of times in recent months. You have to understand, Mr. Spivak, we have a hundred and sixty residents here at Desert Angels. Orderlies were on their way to his room when the accident occurred. We try to respond to all incidents like this one as rapidly as possible—your father rang the call button and it couldn't have been even five minutes later when we got there. We're all very sorry."

"He slipped in his own shit," Spivak said, his voice soft and full of awe. "Gee, that's really something." He stood up and shook her hand limply, then walked away.

Outside, the heat was like a brick wall. He walked through it bent over, trying to avoid the glare of the sun. As he crossed the parking lot he felt the pavement sucking at the soles of his shoes. He tried to remember what his rental car looked like, but all he could think of was the phrase *He slipped in his own shit,* which echoed in his head like a dull gong. There it was, the rental car, a deep maroon something-or-other. All he knew about it was that the air-conditioning worked. What did people do out here, he wondered, before there was air-conditioning? Probably nobody lived here back then. Probably Tucson was just a couple of adobe huts stuck among the cacti and the scorpions. Probably people slipped in their own shit all the time, and nobody was there to clean it up except a few coyotes.

At his next stop, the Marshak Jewish Funeral Chapel on Orange Grove Road, he waited for nearly half an hour on a Roman bench in the cool, marble-floored lobby until Stan Marshak, the funeral director, was free. A receptionist brought Spivak a cup of weak coffee, which he sipped while he listened to the dim sounds of weeping that came from behind the handsome mahogany door of Marshak's office. He stared at a large stainless steel sculpture which hung on the wall across the lobby, and realized after a few minutes that it was supposed to be a menorah. Finally the door to Marshak's office opened, and a huddled family group walked out, gripping each other and sniffling.

Marshak came out behind them, wringing his hands. He was a tall, spare man dressed in an expensive-looking black suit. "Mr. Spivak," he said slowly, his head cocked to the side. "Stan Marshak. So sorry for your loss." He clasped his hands at his throat and stood frozen there for a moment, remorse dripping down over his long, ravaged face. Then the moment passed, and he waved Spivak wearily into his office, which was festooned along its paneled walls with framed certificates of merit from various Jewish organizations.

"Well, I've gone through our records, and the good news, Mr. Spivak, is that your father provided for everything," Marshak began. He let the word "everything" slip through his lips in separate, breathy syllables, as if Spivak's father had shown shocking, unprecedented foresight—the first person in recorded history to ever prepay a funeral.

"Is that right," Spivak said.

"Absolutely." He flipped through a pile of paperwork. "Yes, here it is. Just look at this, will you?" He shoved the papers across the desk. "You see there? Sol Spivak—right there, that's his signature." He tapped a finger on the top sheet. "Everything's paid for in advance. Your father did that several years ago. Burial plot—he even picked out a casket. Will you look at that. Very considerate, indeed." He shook his head and tsked.

"Well, that's good news. I'm relieved—and frankly surprised, I have to tell you. My father wasn't usually one to think ahead."

"Well, you can relax, because everything's been taken care of. Except of course for my fees, and for a few other odds and ends. Your father was orthodox, was he not?"

"My dad? Oh, no. I don't even think he belonged to a synagogue, as a matter of fact."

"Are you yourself a practicing Jew?"

"No, not really. I mean...no. But I know he'd like to have a Jewish burial."

"Yes, of course," Marshak said. "I understand perfectly. We'll make sure everything is done strictly according to Jewish law. So for starters, then, there will be the additional fee to have the body watched until the funeral. That's traditional. Then there'll be the ritual washing and wrapping in a shroud—again, it's traditional. And then there will be the rabbi's honorarium. Traditionally, five hundred is suggested. The cost of the casket has gone up, of course, since your father made his arrangements. Everything's gone up-up-up. The cost of fine woods like mahogany—"

"Wait a second. I thought in orthodox funerals the casket was just a pine box."

Marshak looked up at him under lavish snow-white eyebrows and held the pose for several beats. "Yes. Well. If you'd like to go that route."

"Isn't that traditional?"

"Your father prepaid the cost of a fine polished mahogany casket. But of course you as the surviving son—you are the surviving son, are you not?"

"Yes, I am."

"Well, of course you're free to do what you'd like. These were your father's wishes, but—"

"What are we talking about, in terms of price difference? Roughly, I mean."

"Between the pine and the mahogany? About five hundred dollars."

Spivak sat back in his seat. "Are you absolutely sure my father wanted the mahogany?"

"Oh, yes. It's right here in black and white."

"Well, that's a mistake. I bet he just circled the wrong box or something. All my life I've heard that Jews get buried in plain pine caskets. I've always admired that, you know? It seems so much more sensible than something fancy. *Goyim* go crazy with their polished caskets and open viewing of the dead and all of that. It's disgusting. Who'd want anything like that?"

"So you're saying you want the plain pine? Is that it?"

"Yes. That's definite. Let's go with the pine."

Marshak cocked his head and pursed his lips as he jotted a note of his pad. Then, not bothering to look up, he said, "Fine and dandy. Let's just do a little figuring here, shall we?" At that, he fell into a five-minute frenzy of calculations, scribbling furiously on a pad, muttering to himself, transposing figures onto other sheets of paper, pounding out nervous, staccato rhythms on an adding machine. Finally he rested, and leaned back into the plush leather cushion of his chair. "Well, are you lucky," he said, shaking his head in admiration. "Isn't this something."

"Oh, yeah?"

"Just look at how this has worked out," Marshak announced, and pushed a ruled pad of paper under Spivak's nose. "Now first you'll see I've given you the fifteen-percent discount on my own fee—we call it our Out of Towner Special. It's a little something we like to do here at Marshak—so many of our bereaved are from out of the area. Then you'll notice that I've waived the traditional fee for having the body watched until burial. That one's 'on the house'! But wait, this is the nicest part—you'll notice the fifteen-percent deduction off the standard rabbi's honorarium. A perfectly fine, highly qualified rabbi I happen to know here in Tucson, unaffiliated with any congregation at the present time, looking for a few extra functions to perform. And will you just look at those savings!" He beamed and stroked his wrists, which were long and bony and matted with dark hair, like a chimpanzee's wrists.

The total came to nearly two thousand dollars over the amount his father had already paid. Spivak stared at it. "Did you figure in the savings on the casket?" he asked sharply.

"Of course. Didn't I mention that?"

"No, you didn't. Jesus, that's a lot of money. I thought you said it was all paid for. I thought you said my father had thought of everything."

"And he did, he certainly did, Mr. Spivak. Except for the items we've just discussed."

When he got back to the motel he found Rachel out by the pool and stood sweating over her, blocking the sun, describing to her the manner of his father's death. "I mean, tell me, is that death with dignity?" he asked her. "Is that any way to exit this sphere—this plane of existence? Slipping in your own excrement? Is that a way to die?"

"No, it's not, Leo. It's awful," Rachel replied. She adjusted her sunglasses. "I'm really sorry. I wish you would've let me come along with you. I really wanted to. No kidding. I'm serious—I really did."

"Why? What good would that have done? What would it have changed? If you'd been there, you think they would have said he died peacefully in his sleep, listening to Mozart?"

"That's not what I meant." Rachel shaded her eyes and gazed up at him. "It's awful, honey. They shouldn't have told you. What's the point in knowing that?"

"I don't know. Listen, the funeral's tomorrow, and I don't want you to come. That's absolute. This is my job—he was my father, and it's my responsibility. You're on vacation, I want you to go buy some jewelry or something—maybe something turquoise. Go have a massage or a facial. Pretend you're still in Mendocino." He thought of telling her about the issue of the pine casket, but then decided not to bring it up. What if she told him she would have voted for mahogany?

"Are you okay, Leo?" Rachel asked. "You look awful."

"Well, I'm hot. We're in Tucson, it's summertime. This weather really takes it out of a person. I wish we were back in Mendocino."

"No, I mean—you know."

"Listen, this is my version of grieving. I know it's not the way I'm supposed to be acting, but I can't help it. My dad lived for eighty-five years and now he's dead. Period, end of sentence. And get this: the funeral's going to cost me two thousand dollars. Can you believe that? I don't want to be a bastard about this, but my God, that's a lot of money just to put somebody in the ground." He wiped his cheek. "That's sweat, by the way," he said. "I'm not crying. I'm sweating to death." He paused. "I'm serious about tomorrow. I don't want you anywhere near that funeral."

This was the same motel he and Rachel had stayed in fifteen years before, on their first trip to Arizona. In the wake of Spivak's mother's death, his father at the age of seventy had suddenly gone haywire, quitting his job selling children's clothing and moving to Tucson from Kansas City. "I'm tired," he told them. "I'm sick of the ice and snow, I'm getting the hell out of there." He had next to nothing in the bank, no pension at all, just his pathetic Social

Security and the pittance he'd gained from the quick sale of the house. Alone and friendless in the desert, baking in the sun, over the next couple of months he called Spivak every day or two—mournful, remorse-laden conversations which seemed designed to elicit sympathy and money from his son. Then the phone calls petered out, and when Spivak called to check up on his father in Tucson after a silence of several weeks, the old man seemed transformed. He drawled like a cowboy, spoke of needing to "go get some grub," answered Spivak's questions with "yup" or "nope."

Spivak stewed over this new development for another month, his anxiety mounting, then finally he couldn't take it anymore. "We've got to go down there and make sure he's okay," he told Rachel. "He's my father—I can't stand him, it's true—I've never been able to stand him, even when I was a kid—but now he's the only parent I've got left, and he's turning into Gabby Hayes." So just after St. Patrick's Day, when old drifts of brown-crusted snow were still heaped in the alley behind their house in Winnetka, Spivak and Rachel parked their infant daughter, Elena, with Rachel's parents, the Sperlings (who had flown to Chicago just to babysit), and went down to visit the old man in Arizona for three days.

When he and Rachel got off the plane in Tucson that first time, the air was rich and fragrant with desert flowers, the sunshine so bright it hurt their eyes. The elder Spivak, his face as pink as scar tissue, clomped up to greet them in cowboy boots. He wore a shirt decorated with gold piping and brass studs; low-slug jeans hung beneath his belly, held up by a belt with an enormous silver-and-turquoise buckle, and a well-aged straw cowboy hat rode askew atop his freckled bald skull. "Howdy there," he announced in the same twang that Spivak had heard over the phone.

"Dad?" Spivak asked. He peered at his father carefully.

"Y'all hungry?" his father asked. "Let's mosey on over to the Steak Stampede—I could eat me a hoss." At the restaurant, while they were waiting for their food to come, Spivak and Rachel trotted out their pictures of Elena, but his father fanned through them disinterestedly, then shuffled them as if they were a deck of playing cards, and handed them back across the table. After they'd finished their lunch and the plates had been cleared away, the elder Spivak leaned back into his seat, sucking on a toothpick, and regaled them with stories of old time Tucson, his twang growing more noticeable with every sentence. Finally he suggested they all might attend a rodeo that afternoon. "More fun than a barrel of monkeys," he told them.

"We're not going to any rodeos, Dad. That's out of the question. Look, what's going on?" Spivak demanded. "What's with that hat!"

"Keeps the sun off my head," his father said, shifting his gaze to the floor. "Lotta sun out these parts. Man's got to take precautions."

"Listen to the way you're talking. 'These parts.' What's got into you? You think you're a cowboy? Well, hello—reality check. You're a retired salesman from Kansas City, you're seventy years old, remember? Whatever happened to aging with dignity?"

"Your mother aged with dignity, and now she's dead. I loved her, but she's gone, Leo. She was a good woman. The best I ever knew."

"You don't have to tell me that. I know she was a good woman. She was my mother."

Spivak's father turned his gaze to Rachel. "We lived our whole lives for him—for his happiness," he said, pointing at Spivak. "Leo wanted something, he got it. We made sure he never lacked a thing. We may not have had the fanciest house on the block, but—"

"What's that got to do with anything," Spivak said disgustedly, and shook his head. He'd heard this spiel before, and so what if it was true, or nearly true? It was ancient history! What was he supposed to do, hang himself out of guilt, just because he'd had a decent childhood? Okay, he admitted it freely now: at one time, *many sacrifices* had been made on his behalf. This had all occurred during his childhood, when he was a *child,* for Christ's sake, and hadn't noticed any of it; he'd been too busy watching stupid television shows, playing Capture the Flag and King of the Hill, building model airplanes, blowing holes in the yard with illegally obtained firecrackers, camping out at the neighbors' house, getting sick on candy—he'd been masturbating and learning to ride a bicycle by falling off it repeatedly, hoarding *Mad* magazines and pretending he was James Bond, masturbating some more—and so he hadn't had time to keep a running tally of all the things his parents had done without on his account. So okay, already! He felt bad about it now; he cringed to recall his childhood—the shopping trips during which he'd pleaded for new toys, the tantrums he'd thrown on the way to the synagogue on Saturday mornings, the tears, the *kvetching*, the whining for a trip to Wimpy's for hamburgers even though he'd known well enough that the money for such frivolity simply wasn't there. But what was he supposed to do? Travel back in time, get a job at a glue factory at the age of six, so he could pull his own weight in the family?

"I joined the Elks Club last week," Spivak's father said.

"The Elks? Why?" Spivak shook his head. "What's wrong with the Jewish Community Center? Join the temple, or something. Join B'Nai Brith, why don't you?"

"Listen to you. What are you, Mr. Jewish Culture all of a sudden?"

"I just thought you might like to join a temple, that's all. It's a place to meet people. They've got temples out here. Don't you want to have a place to go on Rosh Hashanah?"

"Why would I want that? Your mother was the religious one, not me. All that *davening* and breast-beating. *Oy, oy, oy!* A bunch of pathetic crap—six million Jews *davened* all the way into the ovens at Auschwitz, look what it got them. Anyway—you can go dancing three times a week at the Elks. And I'm a pretty good dancer." He stared at Spivak sharply now. "You probably didn't even know that about me, did you? My own son, and you don't even know I'm a good dancer. Take my word for it, ladies out here line up to get the chance to foxtrot with Sol Spivak. Widows are crazy about me. Look at me: I'm clean, I take a shower every day, I walk a mile every day at the mall, I do my own laundry, I iron my own shirts. I get hungry, I heat up a Swanson TV dinner. You want to stay back there with all that snow every winter? So stay. I want to live out the rest of my life in the sun. Is that a crime?"

And so the ensuing fifteen years had passed, first one widow and then another, sometimes several of them at once accompanying Sol Spivak to the Elks dances. Spivak had met a few of them over the years during his brief trips to the desert to visit his father; though he fought the impulse, he couldn't help comparing them to his mother, and inevitably found each of them wanting—some were stupid, others bitter and cynical. All of them struck him as desperate: corseted, pinched into outfits too small for them, their faces daubed with makeup, their hair dyed a spectrum of unlikely colors. Still, it was a mystery to him that they put up with his father, who seemed to have decided to use his advancing years as an excuse to seek the worst inside himself—to let go of the rope that held us tied, no matter how loosely, to the pier of decency and respectability. He lied incessantly. He shoplifted until he was caught and given a suspended sentence. He grew a Fu Manchu mustache and wore fake gold chains around his neck. He ran up thousands of dollars on his credit cards and then called Spivak in tears, begging him to pay off his debts. He bought a hairpiece that looked like it was made of yak fur, and insisted on wearing it backwards. He cheated relentlessly on every woman he met, then cried and fumed and cursed them when they left him because of it.

But gradually as the years had gone by, his father's health had failed; the sun slowly turned his skin to burnt parchment, the heat sapped his strength so that nine months out of the year he hardly saw the outdoors at all; his dancing turned to feeble shuffling and then stopped altogether, and in its place the elder Spivak turned to the daytime TV talk shows for entertainment. The yak-fur hairpiece and the fake gold chains sat on the coffee table in front of the couch, gathering dust. His personal habits grew shabby. For days at a time he would eat nothing but crackers and peanut butter, washed down with prune juice. He occasionally lost control of his bowels in the shower, and each time called his son to tearfully confess what had happened.

Along the way, of course, the parade of widows thinned out, until finally over the last couple of years there'd been only Inez, who put up with Sol Spivak through seasons of discontent, as he moved bitterly from one cramped, fetid apartment to another. They saw each other at least once a week, when she drove them to a restaurant for an early bird special dinner (he'd finally given up his driver's license at the age of eighty-one, after creaming a public bus broadside in the middle of the afternoon). Inez called Spivak to complain to him about his father every six months or so. "All my friends tell me, they say, 'Inez, what are you doing with that man? He's no good, he's mean to you,'" she would moan to Spivak. "And so I tell them, 'Yes, I know, you're right, he's no good for me, he's too mean.' He's so mean, Leo. What made your dad so mean? Why does he have to be so bad to me? But then I think he's just so scared, he's lonely, he doesn't have nobody else, you're too far away to help him. So I stick with him. I can't help it. I like him. I don't know why, but I do."

Finally, incapable of bathing himself without falling in the tub, unable to keep himself clean or make any of his own meals anymore, his ever-growing array of medicines a bewildering maze to him now, the elder Spivak put up at Desert Angels, a nursing home in the foothills of the mountains on Tucson's northern edge, where for the last year and a half he'd proceeded to go kicking and screaming down the final hallway of his life, making life hell for the staff of nurses and orderlies as he went.

Tall clouds gathered over the mountains the next morning. Spivak went down for a dip in the motel pool with Rachel before breakfast—the one time all day when it was truly comfortable outside—and it was only when he was back in their room toweling off after his swim that he realized he'd brought nothing even remotely appropriate for a funeral with him. Look at him: he didn't even have a *belt* with him, for God's sake. To hell with it— he wasn't going to go out and buy anything at this point. Why should he? Already they were two thousand dollars in the hole— not to mention airfare for the two of them to Arizona, plus the cost of this motel, plus the rental car, and don't forget the cost of the car and the vacation cottage in Mendocino, all of it nonrefundable, money down the drain.

The best he could come up with was a clean pair of hiking shorts and a yellow knit shirt with a little polo pony over his left nipple. He put these on, then looked at himself in the mirror. "What do you think?" he asked Rachel.

"Oh," she said with a sympathetic frown, and put her hands on his shoulders. "Well, what could you do, Leo?" asked Rachel. "We were in Mendocino when you got the call. What were you supposed to do, after all, go buy a suit on your way to the airport?"

"Yes," Spivak muttered, and gathered his wallet and keys.

On the way to Marshak's Funeral Chapel he tried half-heartedly to recall the prayers he'd learned as a boy, but all he could dredge up were tattered fragments, a shred or two of melody, a few unintelligible syllables. Well, who was he kidding? He'd just have to admit it to the rabbi right up front—there'd be nobody saying kaddish, nobody lighting any *yartzheit* candles, nobody laying any *tefillin,* nobody attending services to honor Sol Spivak's name. The plain fact, Spivak told himself, was that he was a bad Jew. He'd *always* been a bad Jew, even as a child, when at his mother's behest he'd suffered through several years of Hebrew school in preparation for his bar mitzvah. Nothing the rabbis told him meant a damned thing; it all seemed about as profound as a game of tiddlywinks, in fact, and though he recognized that he should be ashamed to feel this way, he wasn't. This was Spivak's sense of his destiny, his lineage: though he had nothing solid to back it up, no hard genealogical evidence per se, he felt sure in his heart that he was descended from a long line of bad Jews, an age-old dynasty of skeptics and know-nothings, eaters of *treyf,* nose-thumbers and back-row snickerers, dregs and dropouts, stretching back through centuries of squalid tenement flats and mud-and-straw-hut *shtetls,* tattered tents in the middle of goddamned nowhere, all the way back to the golden calf itself.

Marshak was waiting for him in his office, dressed in a suit even more funereal than the one he'd been wearing the day before. He gave Spivak a quick deadpan head-to-toe glance, then raised his eyebrows and inhaled through his nose.

"I'm sorry. I didn't bring any funeral clothes with me. I know it's inappropriate. I was on vacation with my wife in California when I heard about my father's death, and this is the best I could do," Spivak said. He crossed his arms on his chest to hide the polo pony. "I was in Mendocino," he said, and then added, "It's gorgeous there."

"Yes, I'm sure it is," Marshak said. "Was your wife unable to accompany you? I thought I understood you to say yesterday—"

"She's back at the motel. I told her to relax," Spivak said. "It's so damn hot out, you know? Anyway, she hardly knew my father. We're not exactly a close-knit family."

Marshak gazed at him silently, his head cocked, and he seemed to be on the verge of a comment of some kind when a knock sounded at the door. He opened it, admitting a florid, pudgy man with receding red hair. "Ah, yes. Perfect. Mr. Spivak," Marshak announced, twirling his long, bony hands around, "may I present Rabbi Evelyn Fink."

Spivak shook the rabbi's hand.

"Not a word about my name, okay?" the rabbi said quickly. He flashed a brief, mirthless smile. "Sorry, I always say that—it's a preemptive strike." Marshak excused himself and left the room, rubbing his hands together as if it had suddenly turned cold in his office. Spivak and Rabbi Fink sat down in slippery leather chairs. "Forgive me, Mr. Spivak. I know you're in mourning and all. I'm just very sensitive about my name," Rabbi Fink said. "I've had a rough life. I'm awfully sorry for your loss. And I'm glad you agreed to let me perform the service for your father. I didn't know him at all, so I'll need to ask you some questions in order to prepare a few remarks in the way of a eulogy." He took out a pen and a scrap of paper.

"Ask away."

"What was he like?"

"He was a jerk."

Rabbi Fink laughed nervously. "Well, well," he said, and clicked the pen a few times.

"You asked."

"Yes, indeed. How old was your father at the time of his death?"

"Eighty-five. He was born in Lithuania. He always claimed that he couldn't remember the name of the town. But my guess is, he just didn't want to think about it."

"And how long had he lived in this country?"

"Seventy-three years. He lived in New York originally, got his start in the garment industry, then moved to the Midwest after the war. I was born in Kansas City, Missouri. Now I live in Chicago—Winnetka, actually. It's on the North Shore. My wife and I have a daughter, Elena. That's some name, isn't it? She's sixteen. At tennis camp up in Wisconsin—Camp KeeTonKee." He leaned forward and before he could stop himself he added, "She's spending money up there like you wouldn't believe. How much can a can of tennis balls cost? You know what I mean? I think she's putting most of it up her nose, to tell you the truth. My wife's in deep denial about all of this. 'Cocaine? Not our daughter!' Oh, yeah."

"Okay. Right," Rabbi Fink said, though his eyes were wide. "Isn't that something. Now, about your father, for just a minute... what was his line of work?"

"He sold children's clothing, wholesale. His territory covered most of the upper Midwest. He didn't enjoy it very much, and so he didn't do very well at it, to be honest. When you don't enjoy what you're doing... well, you know. But anyway, it was a living."

"And his hobbies?"

"My father didn't have hobbies. Well, wait a second. When I was a kid he liked to watch the Friday night fights, the Gillette fights, on television. He'd sit in the den and have a beer and let me take sips from it. He liked to dance, too, although I didn't know that about him until after my mother died. She died of cancer fifteen years ago. They were married forty-two years. It wasn't a great marriage, but it was very long."

"I understand," Rabbi Fink said, drawing big, nervous circles on the scrap of paper.

"No, I don't think you do," Spivak said. "See, the fact is, he really wasn't all that great a father. He was gone a lot, and that was bad, but what was worse was that when he'd come home from a trip, he was usually in a rotten mood, because he wasn't earning a lot of commissions, since he really didn't have much of a gift for sales—and he'd say stuff that really hurt my feelings. He called me a little creep once, when I was about ten. I can't remember why he did it. Nobody'd ever called me a creep before, and to hear that from your own father—well, it was very depressing. Another time, I broke a window with a tennis ball and I couldn't get it fixed before he got home—I was maybe eight or nine—and when he saw it, he told me I wasn't his son anymore. I cried for days."

Rabbi Fink ran his tongue around over his top front teeth, as if rooting around for the remains of his lunch. "That sounds awful," he said. "I'm really very sorry."

"Oh, that's okay. I survived." Spivak fell silent, and sank back into his chair.

"Is there anything you'd like to add—anything about your father you'd like me to know?"

"No. I don't think so. I mean, I don't want to sound abrupt, but he lived for eighty-five years, and then he died. You know? He wasn't exactly cut off in his prime."

"All right, then." Rabbi Fink pulled an embroidered yarmulke out of his pocket and clapped it on his head. "I have a confession to make," he said, wringing his hands. "You opened up to me a bit just a minute ago, so I feel like I can tell you this. This is my first funeral. I'm a little nervous. I've been a rabbi for twelve years, and it's been tough, tough, tough," he said, pounding his fist into his palm. "You think your father hated his work? Well, talk to *me* about on-the-job frustration. I've never caught on. I don't know why. I'll get a three-week tryout at a congregation, and at the end of three weeks they pat me on the shoulder and show me the door. I've been everywhere. You want to know what it's like being a rabbi in Sitka, Alaska? I did three weeks there. I think it's my name, you know? They hear the name, Evelyn Fink—*boom*, they're against me. 'Evelyn, what is that, a *girl's* name?' 'Fink, hey, Rat Fink, Rabbi Rat Fink!' Ha, ha. Everybody's such a comedian."

"I'm sorry to hear that. Don't worry about the funeral. It should be a snap," Spivak said. "Nobody's going to show up, anyway. The notice was just in the paper today, and besides, except for his friend Inez, I don't think anybody in Tucson was still speaking to my dad. He was a hard guy to like. And as for a eulogy, you don't have to say too much. Just say he lived a long time and now he's dead, and that ought to do the trick."

"Well, thanks. You're holding up very well under the strain of your loss, I must say. I haven't spent a lot of time around bereaved families, so what do I know about it? But you seem like you're doing great so far, in the grief department, I mean. I suppose it's because you didn't have a very deep or meaningful relationship with your father, anyway."

Spivak bristled, sensing that his capacity for feeling had been called into question. Meaningful? Who'd said anything about deep or meaningful? "We all grieve in our own way, Rabbi," he said, then he shut up, because he didn't know what the hell he was talking about. What did he know about grieving, anyway? Oh, sure, he'd felt a terrible loss when his mother died—for months afterward he thought of calling her every Sunday, as had been his habit, but then each time he realized she was gone, and he'd have to talk to his father instead, he hung up the phone and sat by it, lost and utterly bereft, tears welling up in his eyes. He'd liked his mother, had even admired her, to the very end. She was a woman of true faith, and while Spivak didn't understand faith, and didn't respect it very much, either, he admired it in his mother, because he saw that it gave her a cushion, something firm and comfortable to lean against in her final days when the pain grew intense, and it let her die with something akin to dignity.

This, on the other hand, was something altogether different. As hard as he tried to summon up grief of a similar kind in response to his father's death, all Spivak could think of was the fact that from now on he wouldn't have to send the old guy any more money. For years he'd been sending his father dribbling amounts, a hundred one month, two hundred the next. It wasn't the money itself that bothered him, he told himself. But then he asked himself: what kind of bullshit was that? Of *course* it was the money. After all these years toiling away at Bowles and Humphries, his salary was still stuck in the high five figures—unlike other guys his age, like Adelman in Media, Kinsella in Accounting, and the Bobbsey Twins, Bob Luther and Bob Delgado from Creative, all of whom were vice presidents already, stockholders in the firm. Christmas rolled around, these guys got smacked with bonus checks that had *Mercedes* written all over them. But not Spivak— no, never Spivak, no bonus checks for him. God, it would feel good to stop writing those damn checks to his father. Maybe now he could start saving for something. He didn't know what, just yet—but he could figure that out later. There must be something out there that was worth having.

Marshak tapped on the office door and then a moment later opened it a crack. "May I intrude?" he asked in an unctuous voice.

"I think we're done in here," Rabbi Fink said. He stood up and put a serious, businesslike expression on his face. "Thank you for your candor, Mr. Spivak. I'm sure you loved and honored your father, and I know you revere his memory. I'll do my very best to convey all of that in my remarks."

"Mr. Spivak?" Marshak said softly, in a voice full of steely tenderness. "I'm sorry to seem abrupt, but we have another service scheduled for this afternoon. Please—this way. I'll show you the family viewing room."

The viewing room turned out to be a low-lit curtained alcove off to the side of the chapel. Through a gap in the curtains, Spivak could see his father's casket up on a platform at the front of the chapel, near a lectern. The casket looked pretty nice, considering that it was a plain pine coffin and obviously cost five hundred dollars less than the one his father had ordered. The wood was as pale as cream, and the casket's contours were smooth and rounded; clearly it had been built with genuine skill and care. But still, there was no denying it: this thing didn't pack the wallop of a polished mahogany casket glinting under the lights. There might as well have been a large price tag on it, $500 LESS THAN THE MAHOGANY! scrawled in bold red letters.

Spivak peeked out a little farther to see if there were any mourners. Surprisingly, a group of them sat there, a sorrow-beaten band of arthritic old *cockers* his father had called his friends. In addition to Inez, there were elderly women in attendance as well—a small sampling of the widows his father had courted in past years. The duffers were a fragile, shabby bunch, just as decrepit as his father had been of late. They were tieless, dressed in soiled double-knit outfits, their shirt collars out over their jacket lapels in the style of Israeli Knesset members. One of them had fallen noisily asleep, his mouth open, his dentures slipping out. The widows were sitting in furious, hennaed, clench-jawed isolation, each one occupying her own separate row. How had these people managed to learn of his father's death in time to come here? They must grab the early papers every morning and search the obituaries for familiar names. Maybe they hoped a buffet would be included.

Inez sat by herself in the front row, her bowed head covered in a doily. She was a plain woman with a rough, battered face. She was weeping now; he could tell by the jerky way her shoulders moved.

"Listen, do I have to stay in here by myself?" he asked Marshak. "I feel a little ridiculous peeking through a curtain at all of these people. My father's friend Inez is out there."

"It's traditional," Marshak replied, and handed Spivak a black yarmulke.

"No, I mean, do I have to? Is it required? Is it in the Bible or something? Thou shalt peek through a curtain at thy father's funeral?"

Marshak sniffed. "Of course not. As with everything else, it's your decision."

"Well, fine, then," Spivak said. He slipped out through the curtain and sat down by Inez.

Rabbi Fink opened the service nervously with a hymn that Spivak didn't recognize. It might have been a soothing melody, but Fink's voice cracked several times as he sang, and at one point it seemed he might be on the verge of tears. Spivak sensed that his father's cronies were staring at him from the pews farther back in the chapel—he could feel their rheumy eyes boring into his shoulder blades—but he didn't care. He couldn't stop gazing at his father's casket. The casket seemed very big for such a little guy; his father hadn't stood much over five-six, and in the last few years he'd lost weight, shriveling like a piece of rotten fruit. Inside that box lay the already-moldering remains of the man whose lap he'd slept in occasionally as a small boy—the man who had taught him the ins and outs of manhood, starting with how to pee standing up. Once upon a time they'd played catch together in the front yard night after night, pegging the ball back and forth under the oak tree for hours, until they were called in for dinner or it grew too dark to see. In the years before baseball games were regularly televised, Spivak and his father would sit together on the couch listening to the old Kansas City A's on the radio, eating peanuts and mocking the anemic voice of Monte Moore, the team's dipshit announcer. Sunday mornings in summertime, they washed the car together in the driveway, squirting each other with the hose. When Spivak was fifteen and developed a mustache, his father showed him how to shave, standing behind him at the bathroom sink while Spivak's mother wept in the doorway. He realized now as he stared as his father's casket that he might be embellishing some of this stuff, blowing an isolated incident into something grander, more enduring—but still, he couldn't be making it all up from thin air.

When Rabbi Fink was done singing the opening hymn, he gripped the podium and stared in wide-eyed wonder at the audience of mourners, as if he'd just realized they were there. "What can I tell you about Sol Spivak that you don't already know?" he asked. "What, finally, is there to say about such a man?" He slipped a hand into his coat pocket and withdrew a scrap of paper, which he now consulted. "That he was from Lithuania, came to this country as a young man, moved to Kansas City, and lived there many years? That he was retired, a single man, a widower? You knew all of that. That for many years he made his living, such as it was, selling children's clothes? You knew that, too, I'm sure. And anyway, what does it matter? He wasn't that good as a salesman, and his career's been over a long time." Inez, who'd already been weeping gently, now burst into tears that seemed ready to tear her to pieces. "He was a simple man, Sol Spivak," Rabbi Fink continued. "Not a good man—no, let's not kid ourselves, not a hero. He wasn't a saint—far from it, in fact. He said things he shouldn't have said, did things he shouldn't have done. And now he's gone." He crumpled the scrap of paper and shoved it back into his pocket. "There will be no plaques in this man's honor. No one will ever pray in the Sol Spivak Memorial Chapel. No one will send their child to college on a Sol Spivak scholarship."

"Christ almighty," one of the duffers in the rows behind Spivak muttered, "what the hell kind of a eulogy is this? Who is this rabbi, anyway? What's his name again?"

"It's a common story, isn't it? Ashes to ashes, dust to dust," Rabbi Fink continued, pounding the podium to emphasize his points. "Whoever heard of Sol Spivak? Nobody. What did he have to recommend himself? Not very much. In a week we'll all have forgotten him."

Spivak could stand it no longer. *"AND YET!"* he cried, rising to his feet as if bouncing off a trampoline. He stood stock-still for a moment in shock, his index finger pointed toward the ceiling as if to emphasize an upcoming rhetorical point. Rabbi Fink stared at him blankly. "And yet—he was an Elk!" Spivak said, his voice calmer now. "That's right—an Elk! Isn't that remarkable? Can you get a load of that? He loved it—being an Elk, I mean—the dancing and all. I thought he was crazy, I really did—but he adored it."

"Thank you, Leo, loving son of the deceased—thank you for sharing that with us," Rabbi Fink said. He flashed a beaming, insincere smile at Spivak, and then opened his prayer book as if looking for the proper place to reenter the service.

"Wait a second. One more thing, and I'll be finished," Spivak said to the rabbi. "I'm sorry, I should have mentioned this to you before, in the office." He turned back to the audience of mourners in the chapel. "Give me just a second here. I think he wanted to be a lawyer when he was a kid. It didn't work out, but that was what he dreamed of when he was young. He told me that once.

Oh, and he loved sauerkraut. It was his favorite food, but it had to be ice cold or he wouldn't eat it. He loved borscht with sour cream, too. And he had a weakness for pretzels."

"Thank you very much, Leo. I'm moved by what you've said, and I'm sure everyone here is moved, as well," said Rabbi Fink. "And I'm glad you felt able to speak up this way." When he saw that Spivak had no immediate intention of stopping, the rabbi shut his prayer book, glanced briefly at his watch, and rolled his eyes.

"When I was a little boy we'd go to the swimming pool at the Jewish Community Center and play a game called King of the Corner," Spivak said. He inched toward the podium now, and rested a hand on it as he spoke. "It was my favorite game. My dad would get in the water at the shallow end and wedge himself into a corner of the pool; he'd wrap his arms around this lip of tile so he had a good grip, and I'd try to pull on his legs to yank him out of that corner. He'd kick and splash, and I'd hang on to his legs and pull. He never seemed to get tired. We'd go for hours, and then whenever I wanted to play King of the Corner again, he'd always say okay."

Rabbi Fink cleared his throat. "Mr. Spivak? Are you finished now? We should move along," he said, and reached out a hand to caress Spivak's shoulder.

"I wish I'd remembered all of this earlier," Spivak said. "I just thought they'd want to know some of this stuff. Every year at Passover," he began—then, when he felt Rabbi Fink's fingers tighten slightly on his shoulder, he karate-chopped at them fiercely until they loosened their grip. "Every year at Passover," Spivak began again, "my dad would go into a big harangue about leaving an extra wineglass on the table for the prophet Elijah. He'd tell me to keep my eye on the wineglass so I could watch Elijah come in and take a sip, and I'd try to keep my eye on it—I mean I'd watch it like a hawk—and somehow every year, every year without fail, at some point late in the seder after my attention had wandered, he'd cry, 'Look, Leo!' and there it would be, Elijah's wineglass, sitting there half-empty. It used to knock my socks off, every year. He did that for me," he added. "He didn't believe in any of it. He didn't believe in a goddamn thing, but he did that for *me*. I don't know why he did. I think he wanted me to believe in something. It didn't work, but at least he tried." Spivak filled his lungs with air, and sighed out a deep breath.

At that moment Stan Marshak burst into the chapel through the back door, clapping his hands. "All right, everybody," he announced, "let all who mourn this man rise now to recite the mourner's kaddish. Up, up, up! We've got another service coming in at half past three, and we need to move forward, please. Let's keep it going, please, and thank you very much!" He glared at Spivak, then at Rabbi Fink.

Biting his lip, his head hung low and his cheeks stinging, Spivak resumed his place in the audience and stood with everyone else. He felt as if he were in kindergarten and had been caught poking Rabbi Fink in the ear with a crayon. It had been years since he'd heard the kaddish—years, for that matter, since he'd stepped foot inside a synagogue—but now as the meager, forlorn group of mourners began hesitantly to recite the words, the melody came back to him quite easily, and the words, as well: *Yiskadahl, v'yiskadosh, sh'may rabo,* all of it dredged up from some bittersweet well of memory inside him—the same place he kept all the Top 40 love songs from his youth. Not so bad for a bad Jew, he told himself. He could hum along, at least, and that had to count for something.

Inez stood by his side, tears streaming down her rough cheeks, leaving black mascara tracks through her rouge. She wasn't reciting the prayer; even with the transliteration spelled out in English on the facing page, how could she hope to wrap her lips around these unfamiliar guttural phrases? It must have sounded to her ears like a fitful effort to bring up phlegm. Spivak put a comforting arm around her shoulder and pulled her closer as he recited the kaddish. She pressed against him, and in a moment it seemed to him that she'd melted into his side.

Although it was late afternoon, the drapes in their room were drawn when Spivak got back to the motel, and Rachel was deep asleep on the king-size bed in the cool darkness. He had to shake her roughly to wake her up.

"I'm back," he said. "I'm an orphan." He sat down heavily at the edge of the bed.

"How was it?" Rachel murmured. She rolled over and looked at him a moment, then switched on one of the bedside lamps.

"I don't know. It was okay," Spivak told her. He swung his legs up and lay back against the pillows, then he arranged his arms and legs just so, and stared up at the ceiling.

"You were gone a long time," she said in a tired voice. "I was worried."

The telephone rang on the nightstand.

"Don't answer it," Spivak said sharply, and Rachel pulled her hand back from the phone. He watched her intently; if she made a move for the phone, he was prepared to intercept her—to break her arm, if he had to.

"It might be Elena calling," Rachel said. "I called today and left a message for her to call. She'll be worried. Let me just—"

"No," Spivak said, and moved between Rachel and the phone. "No more phone calls. Let it ring."

And so it rang. The intensity of his gaze softened; he really wanted to tell Rachel about Rabbi Fink and that lame excuse for a eulogy, and about Marshak and his Out of Towner Special, and about Inez and the other widows and the miserable pack of *joskies* who'd showed up in their polyester *shmattes* to mourn his father. Most of all he wanted to tell her about the pine casket and the five hundred dollars.

The phone kept ringing. "Leo?" Rachel said, and put a hand on his arm. "Honey?"

If he could just get the part about the casket off his chest, he thought there was a chance he might be able to breathe again. He could just blurt it out, make a joke of it, even, and Rachel would tell him he'd done the right thing, he was sure, and he would know she was lying, but he could deal with that part, he really could. The part he couldn't deal with was that she'd know that he'd fucked up once again, and sometime soon he'd catch her looking at him with that expression he'd seen in her eyes before: *Leo, Leo, why are you such a shmuck?* And anyway, what was he supposed to do about it now? Was he supposed to exhume his father's body and confess his sins? Face it: the thing was over and done with. Finished. So why mention it to Rachel? Why even bring it up? What good could it possibly do?

"Leo? Speak to me, honey. C'mon," Rachel said. The phone abruptly stopped ringing, leaving a metallic, echoing silence in the room.

No, Spivak told himself, there wasn't anything to be done about it now. It was too late. And there was no going back, no second chance, no rewinding the tape and getting to do it all again: it was going to *stay* too late forever. Now he could finally get on with the business of living the rest of his life. The only hard part would be learning to breathe with this goddamn weight on his rib cage. The rest of it was going to be a piece of cake.

Family Stories

I had a boyfriend who told me
stories about his family, how an argument
could end up with his father grabbing
a lit birthday cake in both hands
and hurling it out a second-story window. That,
I thought, was what a normal family was like: anger
sent out across the sill, landing like a gift
to decorate the sidewalk below.
In my family it was fists, and direct hits
to the solar plexus, and nobody
ever forgave anyone, but in his stories
I could believe people really loved each other,
even when they yelled
and shoved their feet through cabinet doors,
or held a chair like a bottle of champagne
and broke it against the wall, rungs
exploding from their holes.
I said it was harmless, the fury
of the passionate—elaborate and dramatic.
He said it was the curse
of being born Italian and Catholic,
and that when he looked out that window
all he saw was something rudely crushed.
But what I saw was a gorgeous
three-layer cake fallen open like a flower
on the sidewalk, the candles broken,
or sunk deep in the icing, but every one of them
still burning, refusing
to let anything put them out.

Trying to Raise the Dead

Look at me. I'm standing on a deck
in the middle of Oregon. There are
friends inside the house. It's not my

house, you don't know them.
They're drinking and singing
and playing guitars. You love

this song, remember, "Ophelia,"
*Boards on the windows, mail
by the door.* I'm whispering

so they won't think I'm crazy.
They don't know me that well.
Where are you now? I feel stupid.

I'm talking to trees, to leaves
swarming on the black air, stars
blinking in and out of heart-

shaped shadows, to the moon, half-
lit and barren, stuck like an axe
between the branches. What are you

now? Air? Mist? Dust? Light?
What? Give me something. I have
to know where to send my voice.

A direction. An object. My love, it needs
a place to rest. Say anything. I'm listening.
I'm ready to believe. Even lies, I don't care.

Say *burning bush.* Say *stone.* They've
stopped singing now and I really should go.
So tell me, quickly. It's April. I'm

on Spring Street. That's my gray car
in the driveway. They're laughing
and dancing. Someone's bound

to show up soon. I'm waving.
Give me a sign if you can see me.
I'm the only one here on my knees.

Mélange: A Commencement

I came into this world on the back
of a white elephant
who carried a talking monkey
on the sloped smoothness of her tusk.
The monkey
would riddle the trees with questions,
ask them
how many pears they shed in the time
it took Monkey to somersault from one
end of the cosmos to the other,
and back again, and the trees would respond
But we shed only plums.
The elephant would plod along
wishing to be somewhere else
and hoping that someday
the gods would take
a considerable weight from her limbs.
I sat on her back like an empty bowl
not knowing the difference from
the Where We Go and the Where We Came.
The birds watched us from the tops
of puzzled trees, screeching *Mulatta,*
mulatta, thinking, perhaps, that I was a mule
who should carry the monkey and the elephant instead.
When we reached the river of Where We Are,
the monkey and the elephant
turned into small bitter nuts
that I chewed and mixed
into a marrow I swallowed, a pasty
obligation. As I dove into the river,
I heard behind me the blue macaws calling,
Mulatta, mulatta, as if before me
they knew my name.

My Priest Father's

V-necked, tobacco-colored cardigan pocked with tiny holes
burned by embers of his cigarettes.
He wore it when he'd flung off his collar in the sacristy.

I believe he preferred the beauty of women to the virtue
of sermons. I believe he preferred their beauty to giving
absolution.

A gift from his mother who favored him
in uniform: lieutenant-at-arms in the militant church—
he slipped the sweater on and off during those years

before he met my handsome mother in her smoke-colored dress.
When I mull on him naked, nothing but mystery colors my view.
To think I've seen nothing of him but one photographed face,

the body that made me now stripped under earth where he wears
the western light of stars.

Necessity

John Clare
wrote poems
on scraps
of paper,

erased them
with bread
he ate
afterwards.

When he ran
out of scraps
he wrote
in his hat.

When he ran
out of bread
he ate
grass.

The Fool: A Letter to Paul Hansen

When Bodhidharma
came from the West, for nine years
he sat, face-to-wall.
A student asked old Yang-chi,
"What could this possibly mean?"

"He was Indian,"
Yang-chi replied with a grin,
"he spoke no Chinese."
Chuang Tzu says, "If you follow
dictates of an accomplished

heart, then you have found
a teacher. And who can fail
to find a master?"
When I set out for Yueh,
I never dreamed I would find

myself in shadows
of ancient masters whose trails
wind ever deeper
into dark mountain shadows
before the burgeoning dawn.

"He who knows enough
to stop at what he does not
truly know is there."
Well, old friend, let me be first
to confess to wandering

still. The world is filled
with scholars who do not know
that the poetry
is only glimpsed through the words
like a lover undressing

behind the shoji
screen, her lovely silhouette
mistaken for her
body. Poetry is not
the fact of her living flesh

nor the old longing
stirred in the loins by a glimpse
of neck-nape or breast.
The poem is shaped by words
the accomplished heart holds dear,

and, composed by ear,
say much more than words can say.
Take away the words,
and there is still poetry.
Facts merely get in the way.

I have surrendered
to the mystery of it all.
My face to the wall,
mountains and rivers remain.
I am a fool, Paul, to have

thought for a moment
I could stop the moon mid-sky,
that I could embrace,
if only for a moment,
the moon reflected in your eye.

And yet I persist
as the trail winds more deeply—
as I'm aptly named:
Obaka-san the Pilgrim,
a happy fool following

the light reflected
by the eyes of ancient fools,
crumbling old Buddhas,
Taoist loonies—to the point:
people who are just like you.

The Scarf

A turquoise silk scarf, elegantly long, and narrow; so delicately threaded with pale gold and silver butterflies, you might lose yourself in a dream contemplating it, imagining you're gazing into another dimension or another time in which the heraldic butterflies are living creatures with slow, pulsing wings.

Eleven years old, I was searching for a birthday present for my mother. *Mom* she was to me though often in weak moments I'd hear my voice cry *Mommy.*

It was a windy grit-borne Saturday in late March, a week before Easter, and cold. Searching through the stores of downtown Strykersville. Not Woolworth's, not Rexall's Drugs, not Norban's Discounts where a gang of girls might prowl after school but the "better" women's stores where few of us went except with our mothers, and rarely even then.

Saved jealously, in secret, for many months in a bunched-up white sock in my bureau drawer was eight dollars and sixty-five cents. Now in my jacket pocket, the bills carefully folded. This sum was sufficient, I believed, for a really nice, really special present for my mother. I was excited, nervous; already I could see the surprised pleasure in my mother's eyes as she unwrapped the box, and this was to be my reward. For there was a delicious way Mom had of squinching up her face, which was an unlined, pretty face, a young-woman face still (my parents' ages were mysteries to me I would not have dared to penetrate but clearly they were "young" compared with most of my friends' parents—in their early thirties) and saying, in her warm whispery voice, as if this were a secret between us, "Oh, honey, what have you *done*—!"

I wanted to strike that match bringing out a warm startled glow in my mother's face, that glisten in her eyes.

I wanted to present my mother with, not a mere store-bought item, but a love offering. A talisman against harm. The perfect gift that was a spell against hurt, fear, aloneness; sorrow, illness, age and death and oblivion. The gift that says, *I love you, you are life to me.*

Had I eighteen dollars, or eighty, I might have wished to spend every penny on this gift for my mother's birthday. To hand over every penny I'd saved, to make the transaction sacred. For I believed that this secretly hoarded money had to be surrendered to the proper authority, that the transaction be valid, and sacred; that this mysterious authority resided in one of the "better" stores and nowhere else. So there was a heat, a feverish glare in my eyes (that were said to be on even ordinary occasions strange-staring eyes like a cat's). And there was an eager, awkward motion to my slight body, as if even as I lunged forward I was yet bracing myself, steeling myself, in a kind of physical chagrin.

Naturally, I aroused suspicion in the primly well-dressed women who clerked in such stores. The better-dressed the sales-clerk, the more immediate her suspicion. There were several stores experienced in such a nightmare haze of blindness and breathlessness I was inside, and out, in a matter of seconds before even quite hearing the sharp query meant to intimidate and expel—"Yes? May I assist you?"

At last I found myself amid glittery glass display cases and racks of beautiful leather goods hanging like the slain carcasses of animals. A well-worn parquet floor creaked incriminatingly beneath my feet. How had I dared enter Kenilworth's Ladies Fashions, where mother never shopped? What gusty wind had propelled me inside, like a taunting hand on the flat of my back? The lady salesclerk, tight-corseted with a scratchy steel-wool bun at the nape of her neck and smacking-red downturned mouth, eyed my every movement up and down the dazzling aisles. "May I assist you, miss?" this lady asked in a cold, doubtful voice. I murmured I was just looking. "Did you come to look, miss, or to buy?" My face pounded with blood as if I'd been turned upside down. This woman didn't trust me! Though I was, at school, such a good girl; such a diligent student; always an A-student; always a favorite of teachers; one of those students who is on a teacher's side in the fray, thus not to be despised. But here in Kenilworth's, it seemed I was not trusted. I might have been a little colored girl for my dark hair was suspiciously curly-kinky like moist wires, and inclined to frizz like something demented. You would know, seeing me, that such a specimen could not drag a decent comb through that head of snarly hair. And my skin was olive-dark, not the wholesome buttermilk-pale, like the salesclerk's powdered skin, that was preferred. Here was a poor girl, an ungainly girl, a shy girl, therefore a dishonest girl, a sneaky little shoplifter, just give her the chance, just turn your back for an instant. You've heard of gypsies. There were no gypsies in the small country town of Strykersville, New York, yet had there been gypsies, even a single sprawling family, it was clear I was one of their offspring with my soiled skin, shifty eyes, and rundown rubber boots.

It was my ill luck that no other customers were in this department of Kenilworth's at the moment and so the clerk might fiercely concentrate her attention on me. How prized I was, not requiring the usual courtesy and fawning over with which you must serve a true customer. For I was not a "customer" but an intruder, a trespasser. *She expects me to steal*—the thought rushed at me with the force of a radio news bulletin. What hurt and resentment I felt, what shame. Yet, how badly I would have liked, at that moment, to steal; to slip something, oh anything! in my pocket —a leather wallet, a small beaded handbag, a lacy white Irish linen handkerchief. But I dared not for I was a "good" girl who never, in the company of my gang of friends, purloined even cheap plastic lipsticks, fake-gold hair barrettes, and key rings adorned with the ecstatic smiling faces of Jane Russell, Linda Darnell, Debra Paget, and Lana Turner from Woolworth's. So I stood paralyzed in the gaze of the woman salesclerk; caught between the perception of my deepest wish (until that moment unknown to me) and my perception of the futility of that wish. *She wants me to steal but I can't. I won't.*

In a weak voice I said, "It's for my mother—a birthday present. How much is—this?" I'd been staring at a display of scarves. The price tags on certain of the items of merchandise—the wallets, the handbags, even gloves and handkerchiefs—were so absurdly high, my eye took them in even as my brain repelled them, as information bits not to be assimilated. Scarves, I seemed to believe, would be more reasonably priced. And what beautiful scarves were on display—I stared almost without comprehension at these lovely colors, these exquisite fabrics and designs. For these were not coarse, practical, cottony-flannel scarves like the kind I wore most of the winter, that tied tightly beneath the chin; scarves that kept one's hair from whipping into snarls, kept ears and neck warm; scarves that looked, at their frequent worst, not unlike bandages wrapped around the head. These scarves were works of art. They were made of fine silk, or very light wool; they were extravagantly long, or triangular; some were squares; some were enormous, with fringes—perhaps these were shawls. There were paisley prints, there were floral prints, there were gossamer scarves, gauzy scarves, scarves boldly printed with yellow jonquils and luscious red tulips, scarves wispy as those dreams of surpassing sweetness that, as we wake and yearn to draw them after us, break and disintegrate like strands of cobweb. Blindly I pointed at—I didn't dare touch—the most beautiful of the scarves, turquoise, a fine delicate silk patterned with small gold and silver figures I couldn't quite decipher. Through her pinched-looking bifocals the salesclerk peered at me, saying, in a voice of reproach, "*That* scarf is pure silk, from China. *That* scarf is—" Pausing then to consider me as if for the first time. Maybe she felt in the air the tremor and heat of my blood. Maybe it was simple pity. This utterly mysterious transaction, one of those unfathomable and incalculable events that mark at rare intervals the inner curve of our lives, gratuitous moments of grace. In a lowered, more kindly voice, though with an edge of adult annoyance, the salesclerk said, "It's ten dollars. Plus tax."

Ten dollars. Like a child in an enchantment I began numbly to remove my savings from my pocket, six wrinkled dollars and nickels, dimes, a single quarter, and numerous pennies, counting them with frowning earnestness as if I hadn't any idea what they might add up to. The sharp-eyed salesclerk said irritably, "—I mean eight dollars. It's been marked down to eight dollars for our Easter sale." Eight dollars! I said, stammering, "I—I'll take it. Thank you." Relief so flooded me I might have fainted. I was smiling, triumphant. I couldn't believe my good luck even as, with childish egotism, I never paused to doubt it.

Eagerly I handed over my money to the salesclerk, who rang up the purchase with that curious prickly air of impatience, as if I'd embarrassed her; as if I were, not an intruder in Kenilworth's after all, but a child-relative of hers she did not wish to acknowledge. As she briskly wrapped the boxed scarf in glossy pink paper stamped with HAPPY BIRTHDAY! I dared raise my eyes and saw with a mild shock that the woman wasn't so old as I'd thought— not much older than my mother. Her hair was a thin, graying brown caught in an angry-looking bun, her face was heavily made-up yet not pretty, her bright lipstick-mouth downturned. When she handed me the gift-wrapped box in a Kenilworth's silver-striped bag she said, frowning at me through her eyeglasses, "It's ready to give to your mother. The price tag is off."

Mother insists, *But I have no more use for this, dear. Please take it.* Rummaging through closets, bureau drawers of the old house soon to be sold to strangers. In her calm melodic voice that belies the shakiness of her hands, saying, *If—later—something happens to me—I don't want it to be lost.*

Each visit back home, Mother has more to give me. Things once precious out of the ever-more remote, receding past. What is the secret meaning of such gift-giving by a woman of eighty-three, don't inquire.

Mother speaks often, vaguely, of *lost.* She fears papers being lost—insurance policies, medical records. *Lost* is a bottomless ravine into which you might fall, and fall. Into which her several sisters and brothers have disappeared one by one, and a number of her friends. And Father—has it already been a year? So that, for the remainder of her life, Mother's life grown mysterious to her as a dream that continues ceaselessly without defining itself, without the rude interruption of lucidity she will wake in the morning wondering where has Dad gone. She reaches out and there's no one beside her, so she tells herself, *He's in the bathroom.* And, almost, she can hear him in there. Later she thinks, *He must be outside.* And, almost, she can hear the lawn mower. Or she thinks, *He's taken the car.* And gone—where?

"Here! Here it is."

At the bottom of a drawer in a bedroom bureau, Mother has found what she's been searching for with such concentration. This afternoon she has pressed upon me a square-cut amethyst in an antique setting, a ring once belonging to her mother-in-law, and a handwoven potholder only just perceptibly marred by scorch. And now she opens a long flat box, and there it is, amid tissue paper: the silk turquoise scarf with its pale heraldic butterflies.

For a moment, I can't speak. I've gone entirely numb.

Fifty years. Can it have been—fifty years?

Says Mother, proudly, "Your father gave it to me. When we were just married. It was my favorite scarf but you can see—it was too pretty to wear, and too thin. So I put it away."

"But you did wear it, Mother. I remember."

"Did I?"—that look of veiled, just perceptible annoyance. She doesn't wish to be corrected. Saying, "Please take it, dear. It would make me happy if you did."

"But—"

"I don't have any use for it, and I don't want it to get *lost*."

I lift the turquoise scarf from the box, staring. Admiring. In fact its label is French, not Chinese. In fact the turquoise isn't so vivid as I would have remembered. Fifty years ago, on what would have been her thirty-third birthday, my mother had opened her present with an odd air of anxiety; the luxuriant wrapping, the embossed silver KENILWORTH'S on the box must have alarmed her. Taking the scarf from the box she'd been speechless for a long moment before saying, "Why, honey—it's *beautiful*. How did you—" Her voice, usually so confident, trailed off. As if words failed her. Or, with her subtle sense of tact, she believed it would be rude to make such an inquiry even of an eleven-year-old daughter.

That talisman that says *I love you. You are life to me.*

This luminous silky scarf imprinted with butterflies like ancient heraldic coins. It's the kind of imported, expensive scarf stylish women are wearing today, flung casually over their shoulders. I ask my mother if she's certain she wants to give away the scarf, though I know the answer: for Mother has come to an age when she knows exactly what she wants and what she doesn't want, what she needs and doesn't need. Saying yes, she's certain, arranging the scarf around my neck, tying the ends, untying the ends, frowning beside me at the mirror.

"See, darling? It's beautiful on *you*."

DEBORA GREGER

The Snow Leopard of St. Louis

Something bellowed.
No one manned the zoo's ticket window,
only from somewhere came an echo,
a cry lifted bodily over the fence.

And there was the keeper's little door
at the back of a cage. The well-scrubbed floor,
the animal just a furious blur.
Next door a giraffe somehow stretched *down*

to tongue the leaves shed by mere maples.
It was Sunday, church bells pealing
the birds of paradise from their painted perches.
A parrot asked again to be forgiven.

A floe of cement —no, a whole archipelago
had been poured for the polar bear
who gently snored, granting absolution.
Around the corner, the snow leopard stretched

on a concrete altar. His patient glare
left raw the sacrament of meat.
Flies in procession, vestments aglitter,
a penitent sparrow denying the cold—

the leopard looked prepared to wait
for his native blue sheep to be broken like bread.
The world's highest mountains were missing.
On the edge of the Great Plains,

where was the hut selling tea for the climber,
bitter with salt and rancid yak butter?
Where was the prayer wheel spinning in prayer
for leopard and tracker alike, for the goat

bought in the village for leopard bait?
I turned the corner
like a page of *National Geographic.*

The Bolt-Struck Oak

For they have sown the wind and shall reap the whirlwind.
—Hosea 8:7

1. Labor

Theodore Thompson Genoways, born June 24, 1907

The midwife says, *Bite this strop.* Outside, burn-killed limbs—
once spread wide as the province of God—pile in cords,
sorted from kindling to cook-logs. Lynn tears muslin

into even strips, watching Wallace through the door
drag the jagtooth back and forth. His father totters
the branch until it breaks free in his hand, then points

to the next. The girls drop pails—half-filled with water,
half with silt— swelling dust from under the floor joists.
They pour into a cookpot, now nearing a boil.

Wallace buckles the saw to free it from binding,
but three tines snap. He feels the break, gap-toothed and wet
with sap, then turns. To his father, stacking behind him,

he calls, *Should we save out in case of a casket?*
The midwife wipes her glasses, grips the baby's crown,
whispers, *Now when I tell you, I want you to bite,*

then twists, so the shoulders slip past. When he cries out,
she cuts the cord. His father—in the day's last light—
bends Wallace to the stump, belt arcing like a scythe.

II. Drought

Lewis Cass and Catherine, July 1907

L.C. wonders if it ever rains where she is.
Though he could straighten his arm across the mattress
to touch her side, he knows—like oceans of cheatgrass

choking snakeweed and sage—the sick baby constricts
her roots. Parts of her brittle like winterkilled corn.
The day he chained the team to the dead oak and pulled,

something buried bent, then cracked. The baby was born,
and rootstock snapped like bones till the rough trunk jolted
the ground. At the glass all night, she stared at the hole,

while he lay in his cradle, silent and yellow.
He still never cries, and the doctor says, *Sun's
the best cure,* as if there were somewhere she could go

for shade. She twirls the sawtooth leaf between her thumb
and finger, wishing for the wind's slow whisper back
like mist on the roof. L.C.'s in the barn, truing

planks for a floor. From where she sits, he ebbs in black.
She can't see rills of sweat or him stretch, then loosen
his shirt, or hear—high in the rafters—doves cooing

between thrusts of the plane. He inches a level
down the board's length, squinting. He doesn't see her breasts
pale against the jaundiced child. He squares by bevel,

preferring straight lines to her curves where the boy rests
and suckles. Tonight she undresses by lamplight
and slips into bed. L.C. curls her like a spoon,

murmuring how oak retains the quiet of night
well past dawn, but she dreams of hills thick with fescue.
Curtains draw open, cut clover fills every room.

III. *The Turning*

L.C., Aug. 1907

The baby—still bloated with bile—draws chicken-hawks.
The doctor says flux is normal, just his liver
unsouring, but they circle thick as flies. Dusk: rocks

shift where the windbreak slopes south toward the river.
As a boy, L.C. watched a pack close on a calf—
sick from still water—licking the green from its tail.

He prowls the fenceline, following the smoothbore shaft
like a snout. One coyote snapped the calf's flank. It wailed
like a newborn and buckled. He stiffens, then wheels

back toward the house. Light leaks from each windowpane,
sending lattice shadows across the grass, stunted
and sunwashed gray. In the distance, a cattle train

sounds its whistle, and one of the rocks cocks its head.
He levels and fires—a burst like lightning, flaring
a shadow with ember eyes. The calf tried to bawl

but another shadow-dog caught its tongue, tearing
it from its mouth. Sunup, he'll find the coyote balled
in a bed of Indian grass, clotted and smaller

than he hoped. He grips it by the scruff. Catherine
on the lawn beats dust from the rugs, while the three girls
juggle their brother. In a stand of big bluestem,

he stacks branches around the carcass, cuts and piles
underbrush. Wallace shouts, *Do you need me to help?*
He waves him back to the house, a blue thunderhead

climbing the ridge. He opens the cap on his well
and waits. Catherine steps outside, then yells to the children.
They spin like the living. Let hawks harrow the wind.

Mortal Thoughts

More than your shirt I'm wearing.
More than the wildflowers in the field.
The purple will yield to yellow—

when it turns red I will not be here
to see it. This weight I feel is not
the weight of your body. When I touch

your skin I am trying to remember it—
It is not your skin I need to remember.
Nor this particular shade of violet

flattering the field. When your tongue
entered my mouth this morning I tasted
that flower—I know each year the same

color will return. When I take off
your shirt tonight I will anticipate
the red waiting to overtake the field.

Beginning Chinese

My grandmother is tired. She sits at the foot of my bed and asks where I go. I show her my books, and she smiles at the text for Chinese 101. As I turn the pages, she reads the characters she knows—*moon, noodles, peace, fear*—and asks about those she does not. "We haven't learned that yet," I say.

She considers the drawings at the start of each chapter and discovers a story. There is a spectacled man dipping a horsehair brush into ink and a house with six sons gathered for dinner. She says, "That is the teacher teaching his class. And that is a banquet for a woman who's come back from a voyage; she has brought souvenirs and is happy to be home."

"If my father had had money," she says, "I would have gone to school and learned to read. Reading is good, and teaching is respectable. I would have been a teacher, or, I would have been in movies."

She doesn't have time for the chapter called "Leaving China." She sings a folk song as she returns to her work before the afternoon light fails.

Defining the Lake

It is thicker than a woman's hair.
A boat tipped on its side spills
a gift into the waters. The lake holds
a hundred and two wonders in its still
embrace. A cold wind wrinkles its surface
like a spent sheet. You cannot write on it
the way you do on a wasp's hive. A friend wades out
into the shallows and casts a line. A dry fly skittering
on the face of the water is a trick and a deception.
Listen as the lake sings back hymns and your lies.
Listen to the whisper of its hands. A friend slips
into the water and blurs. He hooks gray boots,
bottles, and a drowned book with pages washed
pale and neat, cool and heavy bodies clustered
beneath the waves, fingers clutching
dangled hair like lake moss.
The lake is a bowl.
The lake is a bowl sailing through land.
It is between here and there and here.

for Tim

Grandfather's Alphabet

the o's of his shirt
the o's of his spectacles, his eyes, and his pupils
the o's of his navel and nipples
the o of his belly

of his face and nostrils
his crown of empty hair
of the caps of his knees, the balls of his heels

o of his watch face and the weep of its hands

of his voice curling into the hall
the bright knob
white light cast by a lamp as he reads the news
the o of the magnifying glass
of the glass holding his tea
o of his surprise

the o of his birth
o's circling the map of his village
of his pond spawning goldfish
maps of absence and desire

of the stove
and kitchen pots he fills and empties and fills and empties
o's of mushrooms and snails, rat ears and lotus buns

of water rings on wooden tables and book covers
of the rotary phone
of bracelets, earrings, and keyholes
of the wedding band I've never seen
o of his sadness

o's of birds spiraling above his head
of his Adam's apple pressing the skin of his throat as he looked up

of portholes he looked out, back toward land and out to sea
o's in waves crumbling onshore

the o's of his sperm and testes
the o of his fear

o's cut by propellers taking him home, then taking him home

of his confession, his forgiveness
of his gifts and his discipline

the o of his wife's womb

of sliced fruit
and the plates on which he sliced them
dark o's of thousand-year-old eggs sliced into soup
of mooncakes, sweet crumbs greasing his joy and palms

the o's of church and planets and restaurant tables
the o of his God
o's in his signature
in his name
my name

o of his blank stars

of California

o of a nightmare

o of his boredom trapped in the yard
of cigarettes and smoke
and blowing cheeks
o in his chest, loosing blood

the o of his birth and mine meeting
the o's in old and of
the o of his breath
the o of his voice

a camera's lens with time passing through
his life passing through
the o's of eyes of needles and blackberries

slow o's through the garden on blind afternoons
of a Chinese checkerboard splintering and all its colored marbles

of love and distance
all things and nothing
of his hat and his urn

Invocation

You came to me first as dawn hauled up on ropes
of apricot above the blackened wall of white pine.

You came from the south, from the highest places,
came down from the mountain running.

You were announced by the crows, the shrill
calls of alarm from the uppermost branches.

You opened your throats in a high harsh singing.
I didn't know what you were and rose trembling

from the deck chair, stood breathless and still
where the woods surrounded me, gathered dark

and darker as if to stall the light.
You came down, two of you: one young and red-bright

the other old, rust streaked with gray.
You pretended not to know me and lay down

beneath a small granite ledge, lay on the fallen
needles, licking light into your fur.

You came to me because I have wanted you.
You came though I had asked for nothing,

because I was full as a river at flood tide
with sadness.

You came to me, rested, and then rose, first one,
then the other, and ran downhill into the morning.

You who assumed the guise of foxes, come again
as you did that morning on the mountainside.

And wasn't that you who came last summer
as whale boiling up from the waters of Jeffries Shoal?

Wasn't it you who came in September as wood duck
over the Stoddard marshes, who flew parallel to my car window?

Come to me again as moose invisible on the night road.
Come the way deer steal across the field at dusk.

Come as raccoon, as coyote. Come carrying your burden
of blood and shadow—

come joyous and light with song, come in sleep,
in the unexpected reaches of the day. I am waiting.

Come red-tailed or black-winged; come fluked
and finned, come clawed and taloned,

renew my breath, come full of the mystery
I am only beginning to know.

Cezanne

is right, the pear is always
askew at the brink, always in danger of falling
straight out of the world of sphere
toward the floor we don't often see, that might be
painted a rosy brown or gray green and still tilt
into the landscape that needs brushstrokes
to complete it, to fill in—but he doesn't always—the blanks.

The Same Apple Twice

I keep remembering how he said
You couldn't bite into one without staining the meat.
Egret ice lily egg bone-china white,
only wounded, streaked by the skin's rich red.
Heraclitus, Heisenberg, a boy up a tree on a farm.
And how they proved uncommercial. *No good for butter,*
no good for pies. You had to eat them.

for Stan Lindberg

Limbo, That Abolished World

For five seconds or so, backwards seems possible,
the heirloom un-be-smithereenable. When the voice
first said gently, "We lost her," Wally roared,
"Then go find her!"
Freeze frame: this is Simon and me at the pier,
alive in some previous hour.
Happy, we were happy beyond disbelief.

Poplar Pond, November

One of the old ones has fallen in.
The pond has autumn's clarity and layering,
leaves afloat and sunken,
sky reflections over the bottom's pebbles and scree.
I make up names for the colors of this leaf—
allol, draeth, breen—
while an ant walks all the way up its stem.

So Far

A wild incipience in the air
as if everything stilled
is deeply active, the night cascading
through the tall pines
until it's in the house.
I don't feel just yet
like turning on the lights.
There's an unlikable bird
chuckling outside the window.
Another bird says to it
tsk, tsk.
The end of summer is upon us.
Our kids are grown,
have entered the venal world
with some of the equipment
it takes to survive.
So far so good.
McVeigh's been found guilty.
My wife's in California, visiting
friends she once was young with
who can always make her laugh.
I've never been the kind
who feels deathly in autumn.
I don't bring home the landscape.
But more and more
it just comes in, presses down,
finds correlatives in me.
The moon's shining now
through the big window.
In the world I can't help

but live in, it seems
the cold and the righteous
are no less dangerous
than the furious, the crazed.
Everywhere, an error
leading to an error.
Everywhere the justified.

John & Mary

John & Mary had never met. They were like two
hummingbirds who also had never met.
—from a freshman's short story

They were like gazelles who occupied different
grassy plains, running in opposite directions
from different lions. They were like postal clerks
in different zip codes, with different vacation time,
their bosses adamant and clock-driven.
How could they get together?
They were like two people who couldn't get together.
John was a Sufi with a love of the dervish,
Mary of course a Christian with a curfew.
They were like two dolphins in the immensity
of the Atlantic, one playful,
the other stuck in a tuna net—
two absolutely different childhoods!
There was simply no hope for them.
They would never speak in person.
When they ran across that windswept field
toward each other, they were like two freight trains,
one having left Seattle at 6:36 p.m.
at an unknown speed, the other delayed
in Topeka for repairs.
The math indicated that they'd embrace
in another world, if at all, like parallel lines.
Or merely appear kindred and close, like stars.

Evanescence

The silhouette of a mountain. Above it
a dark halo of rain. Dusk's light
fading, holding on. He thinks he's seen
some visible trace of some absent thing.
Knows he won't talk about it, can't.
He arrives home to the small winter pleasures
of a clothing tree, a hatrack,
his heroine in a housedress saying hello.
He could be anyone aware of an almost,
not necessarily sad. He could be a brute
suddenly chastened by the physical world.
They talk about the storm in the mountains
destined for the valley, the béarnaise sauce
and the fine cut of beef it improves.
The commonplace and its contingencies,
his half-filled cup, the monstrous
domesticated by the six o'clock news—
these are his endurances,
in fact his *privileges,* if he has any sense.
Later while they make love, he thinks of
Mantle's long home run in the '57 Series.
He falls to sleep searching for a word.

Uncanny

after John Berger

When the beekeeper
who lived in a cabin perched
on the side of a mountain also
a sketcher of rocks boulders
and lone trees beaten sideways
by wind
was visited one night
by the shepherd who lived in the valley
he served him dinner the way Abraham hurried
to greet the hungry angel
when the shepherd reached to pay for so much
wine and conversation skillet potatoes with bacon
the beekeeper pushed the money back
and cursed
You're spitting on my pleasure
the shepherd froze
backed up stiffly
holding an unlit cigarette
tears rolled down his
cheeks then down
the other's in such stillness
both stood *until they slowly raised*
their arms and embraced.

At which point I looked up
with moist eyes
from my subway seat to find
a tall black man neatly dressed
in a new leather jacket and gloves
but with something wrong
with his face huge tears
coursed down both

cheeks behind his sunglasses
it being fluorescent night
he removed to slowly wipe his face
then replace but the tears
kept coming on and he
had to continually remove
his glasses and wipe
his face all done
with no sound and I wanted
to—white and a woman
and in New York—
stand and embrace him.

The Soul as a Body

There's a body inside the body.
It's the form that rises up, immune
to fire. It's the kingdom of nothing
as a body. High nothing! You see
its shell in the mirror, draw back.
Feel ashamed. It wakes in a dream
and speaks in silence. Suffers names.
What do *you* call it? The one as two?
Grain of salt? Eater of seeds?
Behold its raiment as it transfigures.
A threadless garment, force as form.
Fatal shroud. You cannot touch it.
It rises from your groin like a quail
with vertical power. Leaps like a trout
to catch the fly in an arc that spans
the world. There is a medium inside
the body like water or air in which
this other body swims *and* flies, is quick
to disappear, you, yet not you. Each being
a surprise of need's design. Each need
determined by another need until
there's only beauty. The more you dress
it up in a single form the less you see
what you cannot see at first. The less
you know the multitudes contained inside you.
It is a body that has come to you
with a passionate love. That sees itself
in all things. That cannot live without you.

Cleaning the Statue

At seven a.m., nobody's here but me and the pigeons
and a few sparrows caucusing in his hair.
Everyone knows how patient he was.
I talk to him sometimes, but he never answers.
"Good morning, Mr. Lincoln. I'm going to clean
you up real good today."
His hands rest on the chair, yet I've seen him raise a finger
to press home a point, give shape to a story,
the voice, many-stranded, coiled on itself.
Step back far enough and tilt your head,
you'd swear it was Robert E. Lee,
gray-beard patriot but not of this Union,
looking down at you—his eyes,
magnanimous as Lincoln's, follow you into sleep.

There are nights when the rain pleads,
blurred lights awakening on the wet streets. He looks
even larger then, an answer coursing from marble cheeks—
As if he could absolve the dead of the future.
But there is a madness slumbering in people
that demands a conjunction in war. I dream
those long legs bear him away, his footsteps
only an echo. He's reviewing the dead,
the long rows endlessly multiplying.
Even he can't see that far.

Meat Science

I'm remembering the time
you sat on a roof in Wisconsin
to get away for a smoke,
and a drunk senior stumbled
to the edge of the roof to take a piss
then folded his body down next to yours.
Below, a faint sound of drums
and bass throbbed through the house.
"Pigs," said the boy, "are as smart
as we are. Smarter. If you don't
believe me, look into a pig's eyes
sometime. You'll see
what I'm talking about."
His hair was yellow, freshly shorn,
his eyes were blue.
He had graduated that morning
with a bachelor's degree in Meat Science.

You learned all about pigs that night,
feeding, breeding, slaughter. "With this degree
I can go anywhere: Oscar Meyer, Hormel..."
You both looked at the stars, remarked
how the moon glowed, a thin, cool dime
on such a warm night. "I shook hands
with my father this morning. Mom took
a picture of me in my cap and gown."
You couldn't remember the particular
breed of pig he had raised, but it had
velvet ears the size of a man's hand.

Each year there was the day his father
killed a bottle of Jim Beam. Maybe
there was a sickness in the weaning
pigs, or a shortfall in production.
He ran to the barn as fast
as he could, his father bellowing
behind him, swinging a black belt
from one clenched fist.
The boy dove into the pigs' pen
and was hidden by quiet sows,
their ears a cover for his face.
You sat blowing smoke
at the stars all night long,
while the boy drank, and cried,
and shaped his story
into something he could hold.

JOEL BROUWER

"Former Kenyan Parliament Member Arrested for 'Imagining the Death' of President Daniel arap Moi"

—*The New York Times, October 1, 1995*

I imagine him behind a desk big as a Buick, irked
the administration's blocked his hydroelectric
or plastics factory scheme, and the idea, unsummoned, arrives
in his mind: the President's head gone in a cloud of blood.

And then the police are there. They smoke his cigarettes
while he finds his coat, and across town a jailer mops down
the concrete floor of a cell, his radio muttering weather...
It could have happened otherwise: this is just imagination.

The same one which last night handed me, unasked,
a vision of an ex as I watched my wife undress—
her true legs and shoulders haunted by misty others,
a ghost spine arched like a cobra in her back—

while I gawked like a traffic-accident rubbernecker,
half-fascinated, half-ashamed, though my actual hands
were clean as this daydreaming Kenyan's,
each of us innocent as a fresco of Judas on a chapel wall.

My ninth-grade Bible teacher claimed thinking the sin
was just as bad as sinning. This seemed to me untrue.
Who was wounded when I pictured the class bully stabbed,
or dreamed my drama teacher nude and willing?

What delicious lack of consequence! What fool would refuse
to swap for it their citizenship in the tangible?
Certainly not our Kenyan un-murderer, now lashed to a chair
in his cell. He imagines himself, let's say, in Florence,

about to emerge from the Uffizi into a plaza stunned
with autumn's blaring sun. See how he pauses at the threshold?
Each time he steps over, the truncheons of the actual
blast again like an avalanche across his broken legs.

WILLIAM LYCHACK

The Old Woman and Her Thief

O n her deathbed, as she drew what were to be her last breaths
on God's green earth, the old woman made a confession so
terrible to her husband that—even under circumstances as
solemn and sorrowful as these—he could hardly take the secret as
true, let alone forgive her for it. He listened by her side, as if
struck dumb with a club, and when she pressed her lips tight
against admitting anything more and a silence had passed, a long
silence in which she could hear herself swallow away the brackish
taste in her mouth, the taste like wet pennies off the street, just
when she expected the final lifting of the veil to all her life's mean-
ing, the old man hiccoughed.

It might have been the fever in her mind, but she could not
accept this to be her life's reward, and she lay there and blinked
her eyes and half expected her husband to cough up an olive pit.
She watched for his lips to purse and spit an inky stone into her
hand, but only the startle of his hiccoughs came, haphazard and
loud in the room. She could feel each jump telegraphed through
the bedsprings to her, and finally she asked him to go drink some
seltzer water. She lay flat and let her eyes close to the dim room
and tried to savor the slow lift and release of each breath in her
chest, and on into the night she lay at rest and at peace.

But she did not die.

Contrary to all they had expected and provided for, in three
days' time the old woman was sitting up in bed and answering
her mail. Scattered about her lay books and dishes and flower
arrangements, bowls of ripened fruit, her little radio and reading
lamps. The curtains and windows were opened wide. And on the
morning of the fourth day the doctor clocked his tongue and pro-
nounced, almost begrudgingly, that she was quite recovered. The
undertaker came and rolled the casket and wreaths out of the old
couple's parlor, where she was to have been laid out, and the
man's cologne lingered so long after him in the room that her
husband lit matches to kill the scent.

Improbable as it became, in two more days the old woman's appetite for chocolate and red wine returned. And her husband knew she was truly well when she asked for a pot of coffee and a bundt cake. As he ventured to the bakery, he caught himself whistling—it was a brilliant spring morning, after all, and he breathed in the cool air like water and stopped to look out over the hills in the distance, the clouds driven across the sky by the blue clear winds that never touched the ground, and all the trees in leaf and flower, and the traffic of people out walking and working, the report of hammers and whine of saws, the spring birds on the grass, the wet grass in the sun the color of old yellowed silver—and on he went walking for her cake, the thought dawning on him that soon she would be up and off to the market herself, lunching with friends and shopping for groceries, everything just like usual, her Tuesday bridge ladies, her Thursday museum committee, her Friday reading to the blind.

The old man's heart became divided after his wife's almost being carried off. On the one side, all his prayers had been answered in full: his wife alive, their world restored, and the warm sun of another spring upon them. What more could he ask for? And yet, in ways he couldn't help, her confession of the thief lay heavy on the other side of his heart. And this half grew increasingly heavy as the days passed. He began to fancy that he had somehow been tricked by life, a thing he had never before thought possible.

Perhaps as a consequence of this division in his heart, or as a result of the wear of his wife's illness put upon him, or even the peculiar strain of her growing wellness upon him, or the gout in his ankles when it rained, or the ceaseless passing of friends and family and whole ways of life, or perhaps it was the troubled rags of feeling old and dull to the world...whatever the reason, all the things in his life grew increasingly strange to the old man. He would glimpse—or would think he had glimpsed—fruit bats hanging folded with the coats in the closet, turtles in place of pillows on the couch. A pair of boots became muskrats under the bench in the hall, then they were dachshunds, and then, a step closer, they were boots again.

As the days passed, the old man went around braced against the world. He didn't know if he believed what he saw or saw what he believed. Was it what you saw or what you thought you saw? Or was it that what you believed in your mind was what you saw in the world? He didn't know the way he used to know, or thought he had known, and it exhausted him to chase his tail like this. He often had to lie down on the daybed and close his eyes for fear that the truth of the world would be revealed to him. He didn't trust his heart could take it.

On the face of it, of course, the man and his wife were destiny's darlings, not so much the envy of the little mountain town as its collective hope. You would have to be blind not to see the care and craft of the old man's silver shop. Not to allow that the woman's reprieve from death smacked of miracle and meant she had purposes unfinished in the town. And despite her years and her children all far-flung, wouldn't anyone say—among the many things people said—that the old woman appeared more radiant and unshakable than she had in months, if not years?

And when she walked into town, she looked less frail in her summer frock than anyone could recall, her basket on her arm as she went, her hard heels on the sidewalk. And everyone who stopped her on the street told her how impossibly glad they were when they heard there'd be no funeral.

Truth was, she said (and quickly touched wood), she'd never felt more, well, sprightly.

And they said yes, wasn't *sprightly* just how she looked? And they would hold her away at arm's length and say how they wept for joy. Then they would bend close and ask had she gained weight and snuck off to a spa? What, they whispered, are those new teeth?

The old woman would blush to the roots of her white hair and throw back her head, brim with the pleasure of a schoolgirl, really, and she would switch the basket of collard and turnip greens to her other arm and keep smiling. "Oh, now," she would say, "come sit 'n' tell me how you've been."

And they would sit to lunch and gossip in the sleepy shade of the market's trees, a drift of carnival music turned from the blind organ grinder, to whom she read on Fridays, and whose swift little squirrel monkey tumbled through the square with his jingling

pouch of dimes and nickels—everything really was like usual—
the pranks of the monkey, the storm crabs for sale in the cages,
the ice and fish and roasting nuts and seeds, the smell of burnt
sugar and salt, and the warm coins in her one hand ready to give
to the laughing monkey, her wallet clutched tight in the other,
because she knew how the monkey, too, was a thief.

Home from the market she walked with her basket of greens
and dinner sausage, a newspaper packet of sunflower seeds and a
bottle of red wine, and the notion to tell her husband of all the
household scandals she had heard and of how she had watched
the monkey sneak his tail around a little boy and tip the boy's cap
over his eyes. And as she went toward home she watched the sky
for stray birds and for her old lost-to-the-world Romeo.

The sun settled behind the trees, and she stopped in a small
garden park and set down her basket and rubbed the aches out of
her hands. In the fountain a copper goose spit water up over its
head onto its back. She waited and watched the sunlit fingers of
the highest tree branches. And softly she whistled his name, rus-
tled his seeds against the newspaper, and again more boldly she
called to him.

The air went powdery toward dusk, and she heard the slow ring
of the vesper bells, and still there was no Romeo. She knew much
better than to hope, but each stir of shadow in the damp air made
her turn and call his name and see and know, despite her best
hopes, that her thief was not there.

The old couple's history came back to them, if it returned at all,
like a story they had heard about or read about somewhere long
ago, the memories scarcely their own anymore, unspooling about
them like rhymes for children. Once upon a time, and the old
man—a young man then, still sticky with the things he touched
in life—would go walking in the Lost Woods near his boyhood
home. And this once he came upon a bird's nest in the path. In
the leaves lay a crow, black and folded open, its feet cut off.

These days were days, back then, of great superstition and
antique cruelty, days where local farmers poisoned whole cribs of
corn to feed migrating birds, the birds thought to be omens of
famine and death. For many years, you could pay your taxes with
salted owl's eyes and crow's feet. Springtime brought festivals to

the little towns, where cannons shot nets over fields of birds and children ran to club the struggling beasts with ribbon-tied broom handles. Many birds grew skittish over these years and learned not to sing. Some were thought to fly out to sea to become fish. And fewer and fewer returned each season, yet it was true that afowling parties still combed the woods every weekend and holiday and shook and chopped nests down from trees—no eagle, goose, or crane, no crow or lark escaping unharmed. All that remained of some species—the Scarlet Hurry Hawk, for instance, or the tiny Skittlelink, who laid eggs smaller than jellybeans and sweeter than marzipan, or even the Passenger Pigeon, easily the most numerous bird on earth, so prolific its flocks hid the sun for hours on end, the cooing and the whirring of wings so loud that the firings of a gun could not be heard—these birds had only their names and the faded specimens behind the smudged glass of the museum cabinets.

But once upon a time, when the old man—a young man—came across the nest with the crow like an umbrella, the man couldn't take his eyes from the perfect circle of twigs and sticks, at the broken eggs and the glint of tinsel in the cup of grass. And whenever he thought back to this, the old man would see himself standing mesmerized by the milk-green egg in the hold of the nest, one egg as smooth as a moon opal, and as empty and marvelous.

He would remember not a speck of sound disturbing the woods, the quiet columns of trees, the pools of light falling on the path, falling as snow falls when there is no wind. And when, as from a dream, the man awoke and removed his sweater and stooped to wrap the nest, he heard leaves rustle above him. And as he carried the nest back through the woods, carried it like a boy carries a bowl full of soup, he hoped to high heaven that his young bride at home would know what to do with a thing such as this.

Hatch and raise him—was it ever a question?—into a silk-black crow, so perfectly black he moved like oil. Their orphan Romeo, they would keep him safe and teach him to speak and fly and to eat at the dinner table. And he learned to waltz and purr on the outstretched paws of the cat, and in the parlor at night the man would teach Romeo to sing like the nightingale, like the chaffinch, like the sparrow, like the gentle playing of the late-night radio, the piano and the soprano so like birds themselves. And with her knitting halted in her lap, the woman would watch Romeo on her husband's knee, the bird's knuckle-skinned feet grabbing the man's trousers, her husband's eyes closed and head tilted, the bird singing and looking back and forth to him and to her, as though they were tossing something between them.

And in the mornings, after the man arose and washed and readied himself for the silver shop—where day after day he hammered the town hallmark into the clattering piles of knives and forks and spoons, so many spoons you would have never imagined mouths for all the spoons—Romeo would fly alongside him as he walked the road to work. And after the bird hurried home to the woman, all the rest of the morning long she would tidy the house and chatter on to her Romeo in what would start out as gladness at his safe return to her and what would amount, in the end, to a steady pour of loneliness.

By the time their children arrived—two boys, two girls, each a year apart—and by the time the children were half grown and half out the door and married and moved away, many things had come to pass in the couple's life together, many things in what had seemed to the woman just a heap of idle days, days scarcely strung along together where not a thing appeared to happen or change or move and where time, if it existed at all, was the thinnest of strings suspended and invisible, with no end to hold the beads of days which slid clean off the skin of the world, as if they had never really been, or better still, as if they had always been, fleeting and eternal both.

She couldn't quite get her head around this paradox—of time's being something entirely different than her experience of it—nor did she try particularly hard. It struck her simply that the old man's silver shop had always put the tableware in homes this side of the mountain. And no one had ever before read to the blind until she was there to read on Fridays. It was all like asking when Romeo had become her thief exactly, or why it had been kept a secret. Romeo had not so much learned to steal as he had forever stolen.

Just as sure as the sun crossed the day, the old man would arise and wet his head and go to work each morning to heat and shape the sterling bowls and caldrons and the endless and loud piles of cutlery. And each morning Romeo would fly along with him and perch from tree to tree to sing the songs of the whippoorwill, the bullfinch, the forktail, the bluebird, the naked-throated robbybell—it was a long walk—the songs of the whiskey-jack, and the waxwing, the waxbill, and as the man unlocked the door of his shop, Romeo stood balanced atop the roof's peak, singing his catalogue of night lieder from the radio. Then, when he caught the first sweet whiffs of coal smoke from the chimney, Romeo would start home to the woman, who had already seen the children off to school and sat on the porch with her coffee and cake.

He knew she would scan the horizon of trees for his windtossed silhouette flying safely home. And always he would come to the porch and walk his nodding walk, his toes clicking on the wood; he would bow for her to come scratch the nape of his neck and to rub his feathers against the grain, as so he liked, and he would begin to purr. And when she reached out her hand to him, palm up, Romeo would open his beak and place into the cup of her open hand a child's jack, or a bullet shell, a long necklace of pearls with a gold hasp, an earring, a heavy brass plumb bob, a crucifix, a pair of golden mustache scissors...

Each became a gift picked special for her, and the best of these prizes set to motion the scandals she brought home to her husband from the market each day. An eternity ring from the stable boy, the young man disappearing with the ring, his employer's horses falling ill and nearly dying from, of all things, grief. A gypsy pendant said to be a nail from the Cross, the caravan leaving a bitter curse on the town that would scatter all the children to the winds far from home. There was a heart locket, which undid a promise and the lives of two young lovers. And there was the pair of platinum-rimmed eyeglasses taken from the jeweler, the man stumbling to his death out the open window of his studio, a scatter of uncut diamonds cast about his body in such a way that people said he must have become, through long practice and labor, the very stuff of his art. Even the holy priest requested that the undertaker eviscerate the jeweler for hidden gems. In the weeks that followed, children would throw stones at the glass blower to see him shatter, the banker would snip off his little finger with a cigar cutter, the aged silversmith—the old man's mentor—would be bound to trees in the woods, his veins opened so that his blood could be drawn and cast into coins. And the town would never rise out of its shame to breathe a word about the fate of the quiet vintner, Lord rest his soul.

Many years passed in this way—the town secrets tied to and tied by a crow and a thin old woman—and anonymously she parceled her hoard to the museum and library and church charities. She gave to the organ grinder and quietly stirred the silver brooches and rings into her husband's foundry pots, which cooked in the center of his shop. And though she wanted only to tell her husband the real secrets beneath the secrets she brought home from the market, she didn't know how to explain so he would understand.

Even when she confessed and felt the weight of the world lifted, she couldn't dare tell how she held the picture in her mind of Romeo flying through the woods and town—a complete shadow—flying over the trees and streets for that glint of gold that he could bring home to her. She fell in love with that idea, fell in love so deeply that no matter how wrong and weak and terrible she knew it was, no matter that the longer she kept the secret the more highly keyed it seemed to become, until even a lowly tin soldier or a bell off a cat's collar was enough to break her heart for an entire afternoon, she fell in love so deeply that nothing could bring her to deny herself her thief, nothing could bring her to deny herself the idea of him flying through town, a chain swinging in his beak.

And when all the years had passed, when even Romeo's feathers had gone lusterless and grayed, the old man still worked the spoons in his shop and Romeo still flew as her thief. And at night, as she tucked the bird into his cage to sleep, Romeo would purr and coo back to her the voices and soft words of each of her children, the sighs and coughs of her husband, the squawk of the kitchen door being opened and closed, her own voice saying "Pretty bird."

And she would whisper, "Yes, Romeo, pretty-pretty."

The old man no longer slept well, especially during his wife's illness, and he had taken to napping on the daybed. He could sleep during the short winter's days with the noises of the street to distract his mind from the bellows-like wheeze of her breathing and the pauses which he feared would not end.

When she had first taken seriously ill, their children all swarmed home with their caravans of spouses, pets, children, toys. And yet, as their old mother's illness dragged into the spring, they begged off and returned to jobs in scattered cities far away, each traveling with silver goblets and cutlery from the front hutch and sideboard. And as the nights passed, the old man sat in the room alone again with his sleeping wife, listening to her labored breaths, and he thought it funny how none of the children had mentioned Romeo's absence. He thought this showed how deeply they grieved the imminent loss of their mother; but later, in the smaller hours of night, he took it more as a measure of the distance and time between them. He didn't know what to do with the sadness he felt when, in the sober bright of the next days, he could see that not one of their children had become a friend to them, that he and his wife had passed all their years with his apprentice, with his wife's bridge ladies, with each other and work and Romeo, with the town market.

He didn't do anything with this sadness, unless allowing it to wash over him was doing something, unless traipse-wandering through the Lost Woods with packets of seeds counted for something. And though he feared him dead, the old man whistled up to the trees and looked for the bird's crushed bones amongst the ferns and the wood-roses, and all the woods held quiet around him, the clouds in the sky through the leaves far above like the breaking surface of the sea, the spears of light as though through water. And with a swell of sadness again and of sympathy—for the birds and his wife and Romeo and his friend the vintner and the numberless sufferings in the little town he felt sympathy, as he would for himself and his hunched-over life of silver and chasing tools—and there in the woods the weight of the crow seemed to rest on him, that unmistakable weight of Romeo on his leg, light as a bird is light yet isn't light, and the old man found himself singing the night songs until his throat was red.

No Romeo came to him, and with his boots wet-through from pushing aside the morning ferns, the old man started home and a flash caught his eye, a baby's bracelet. He brushed the dirt from it and hurried home all full of pride—sticky as pine pitch again— smiling to hold the little prize out to his wife. She would fly to him, he thought, her eyes all alight for him. But instead she screamed so fiercely that he thought she was in pain and dying right there. She clutched at the bracelet, and he tried to cover her with blankets. "What have you done with him?" she cried, her face tight and scoured-looking. "What've you done? Where is he?"

Her words fell on him like mallets, and the old man stuttered back to her how, in the woods, by chance, he'd found the bracelet under a fern, with other ferns. He pointed to the toes of his boots, as if he needed more proof, and took mushrooms from his coat pockets and cupped them in his hand. He held out a tiny pine cone from his breast pocket.

She looked at his feet, the brown boots dark with wet, and she lay back heavily and brought the gold metal to her face, touched it to her tongue, and tried to catch the humid smell of Romeo on the bracelet. She didn't look to her husband, even when he sat down beside her on the bed and took her hand and toward his weight she tipped slightly and poured—until she closed her lips again tight against anything more—her life's confession out to him.

The old man would go to his grave wondering what more he could have asked for: his wife recovered, their world spared, spring upon them. And yet, as the days passed, he found himself unable to be roused from bed, unable to venture far from the house, and many mornings he would lie in bed, staring at the window, trying to listen to his heart as he would the sound in a seashell, and his mind would flit in and out of dreams and memories, the difference between the two no longer important for him.

What's more, the old woman had become well with a vengeance. Her appetites restored and habits renewed, she went out each day and bounced as she stepped down the sidewalk into town. The old man watched her go, her white hair shining in the sun. And he watched, and kept watching, the empty street. A little breeze came in the window, and the curtains waved up and bowed down slow before him. And when the old man stepped outside into the light, he thought diamond necklaces hung on the wet grass. Or had the house windows shattered? Could the dew be the tears of stars?

Stand up straight, old man, he said to himself. Enough.

And he would turn from where he stood and go back inside to lie down on the daybed and look at his dry, spotted hands until he had chased himself inside out. He looked through the window and curtains and was back to watching as the sun—with all the patience and fortitude of the mountain and woods—did its work of turning the shadows of the lamppost and the tree up on their ends, of holding those shadows there, and then of gently laying the shadows out again opposite. And dusk brought the vesper bells and the approaching click of his wife's heels on the walk, the heavy creak of her basket filled with dinner greens and fruit, the old man's heart chanting that the trouble's no trouble, the trouble's no trouble...

And over dinner and wine he listened as she chatted cards and told how, in the market, the monkey tipped the hat from boy and how last week she read a pirate story to the organ grinder and could swear the monkey was weeping when the parrot in the story was captured by the mutineers and was made to stand trial against his captain.

In the living room, late into the night, they sat and listened to the radio. Sometimes they would remember the past for one another—their marriage trees as saplings, their trip to Barcelona—but mostly they just remained quiet together in the room, the man absently turning through a book of still life paintings, and the woman's knitting halted on her lap as she stared at the dark empty windows, the soprano on the radio rising onto her toes, her piano slowly falling to the floor—and coming to rest—like a leaf.

"You know who'd've liked that song?" he asked her.

The needles in her hands began to tick together again up and down, and she looked over at his finger running along the edge of a page, and when she raised her eyes to his, he winked. She dropped a stitch and pulled out lengths of yarn from the skein tumbling on the floor.

After the next song—a waltz that had been popular when they were courting—she said, "That wasn't so bad, either, was it?"

"Incredible," said the man. He hummed just slightly and closed the book on his lap and watched as she knit. He lay aside the book. "Know what I'd most like to be in my next life?"

"What's that?"

"A musician and play like that."

"I'll see what I can do," she told him.

He sat down. It was a joke and he had been sitting right along, but he sat down even more, as though forcing air from his body to touch bottom. He sat heavy in his old bones and looked at her. He had been looking at her all along, all his life he had been looking, but he looked more—and she was a wolf with knitting in her lap, then she was a little girl frail and lost in gray hair and old lady clothes, knuckles swollen, and then again, what, old man, who was she besides the only one you'd ever love in this life of clattersome spoons and singing crows?—and sudden and soft he had landed in this chair in this room in this night. A smile floated up to his face all by itself, he could feel it rising in his cheeks and eyes, this brightening, and he found a laugh starting out of him, and soon he was laughing in that big easy way some men have, men of the moment who can shake off their troubles by the door and let out that three-cheers-to-fiddle-player's laugh, which rattles bottles against barroom mirrors.

When she started to say something, to apologize, he rose to his feet and took her hand and led her out to the porch, where they stood together and watched the night, the black trees, the moon, the stars so close you could stir them with a finger, an animal in the leaves under the porch. And they closed up the house and went to bed, it being so late, but the man had a tickle in his throat and couldn't sleep in the quiet and began coughing. He got up and went to the kitchen for seltzer water and lemon. In the silvery moondark he sat at the kitchen table and cleaned his teeth with a toothpick.

That morning—the sunlight streaming into the house through the curtains, the birds outside singing—when she went to the room with the daybed, she carried a tray with their coffee and juice and muffins to him and found that, during the night, he had died.

There was consolation to be had in the busy details of the wake and funeral, in the playing of host to friends and family, in the attending to train schedules and sleeping arrangements. An odd, quiet solace also crept into the old woman's answering of sympathy cards and her writing of money orders to the churchyard and stone carver and undertaker, that cologne of his carrying the

memory of every death in town. And at every other corner some-
one waited to keep her distracted with lunch in the market, with
gossip, with invitations to dinner. It struck her that everyone—in
a fit of pity—conspired to let her never be alone again.

And as the old woman withdrew from them all, they would talk
of how she carried her grief—so sad, they said, silently worrying
over their own ends—and they would turn their leading questions
to the organ grinder, for he was believed to have second sight.
What with his accent and those cream-clotted eyes and the little-
man monkey over his shoulder, who would not look twice at the
man and feel the cool, root-cellar air of an oracle about him?

Well, the bridge ladies, for one, couldn't care less and com-
plained mostly about forgetting their cards. And of what concern
was it to the museum committee, their anonymous donors all but
vanished, bankruptcy staring them in the face so close that by the
middle of each month they had to rent out their halls to wedding
and birthday parties? And nothing ever seemed to touch the
organ grinder, either, to whom the old woman still read on Friday
mornings, even though she wondered if he still cared to listen. It
seemed to her that he would awaken only when she stopped read-
ing or digressed from the story.

"Excuse me," he would say, "but it says that for real?"

And she would smile over to the monkey—who crouched so
attentive in his little mustard-colored suit—and she would return
to the page and clear her throat before she picked up from where
she had broken off. The man wanted only ghost stories, of late,
and the more avenging the justice, the more haunted the con-
science, the better. And the monkey would snort at each turn, at
each squeaking door and midnight romp he would somersault in
his seat, and a dull guilt would tie up the old woman's neck, as if
her reading held within it something mildly illicit. With the
bright morning and the chirping birds, the stories of grave rob-
bers or shipwrecks seemed to her like brandy at breakfast.

But to see the monkey squirm in his seat and begin to clap as
she reached lunchtime and the end of the tale, where the ghosts
all marched onto the waves to their foggy ships, that was fine.
And as the monkey clapped, the organ grinder opened his onion-
white eyes. "Brav-o!" he said. "Brav-o!"

And she whiled away the afternoon with lunch and coffee and

the organ music in the market, the crabs and roasting seeds and fruit stalls, and the water-cool shade of the trees by the benches where she sat and met the usual passersby, whose pity she despised more and more with each smile and new scandal that came her way. And closer to evening, the old woman sat out on the porch with her wine and chocolate and the sun behind the trees, the branches in strong tangled shadow. It was autumn but the light was warm, and she waited for night to fall as birds flew home to their nests. She carried sunflower seeds out of habit, but she hardly ever watched for her Romeo and his soft return, which she had once seen in her mind so clearly, a smudge of black against the horizon, his raucous flying home at one time so fully imagined to her, it seemed already fulfilled somewhere—the roll of his wings, the fanned spread of his tail, the silky hiss of his feathers, the tick of his feet upon the wood porch.

"Hello, bird," she said to a grackle in the shrub, who tipped his head and looked to the seeds she was holding out in her hand.

She said, "Take some," and the bird squeaked a rusty gate of a song and flitted to a branch in a tree, slightly higher, and the old woman stood and came forward with her hand out. When she was close enough to see how his eye shone yellow and how his black feathers glossed purple, he whetted his beak and then twittered to a tree near the street and turned on his perch and watched her again. She was on the sidewalk and with him, past the post office and fire station and market, her bird before her in the tree just distant, past houses and smells of dinner, past the cemetery and church, she followed tree by tree until they were beyond even the railway station and he was gone from view.

The sky darkened left to right over the town, over which the moon also rose, nearly full, bright and clear enough to cast shadows. And into the gutter the old woman pitched the seeds from her hand. Beyond the shuttered market stalls, she could see the glow of lights against the museum façade. Every light must have been on—the whole place alive with light—but not a soul stood on the steps at the entrance, no guard or coat-check with his arm draped over the ancient lion in the foyer. Music, yes, and the muddled drone of voices and glassware from the ballroom, like some empty and haunted ship, the old woman feeling close to invisible as she turned at the suits of armor down the long side hall, draped ceiling to floor with royal tapestries, the music and voices fading behind her, only the occasional burst of a girl's laughter flying after her, as though released.

At the end of the hall, double doors with portal windows stood dark, and when she pushed them, all their heaviness swung easily and silently aside and opened onto her favorite of all rooms in the museum. The doors closed behind her and she let her eyes adjust to the dim light of the room. All was quiet. And slow and gradual, the sponged clouds came clear on the high-domed ceiling, and once more she was in the company of the gulls and kestrels suspended and the wandering albatross hanging there on wires above her.

She walked beneath them—the big wheeling birds under clouds—to the wall of bright cases, each holding a bird as posed and half-real as a painting of a bird, a painted bird under smudged glass and glare of lights. The last known Passenger Pigeon, who had been named Martha, sat alone in her case and stared with her glass bead eyes at the room, at the woman, at the other birds. And next to her, as remote as the rest, the Bourbon Crested Starling sat on a branch, holding a cricket in his beak forever, accounts telling how this bird could be batted down with a yardstick, it being so trusting and tame. And the old woman came to the Great Auk and could practically hear him say his name as she stood before the antique specimen, his feathers soft as velvet, his wings spread, her hand on the glass as if he could be frightened away. She passed the Mysterious Starling and the Paradise Parrot and the Rodriguez Solitary, who looked so delicate and alert that she had to remind herself that these birds—the Spectacled Cormorant, the Chatman Island Rail, the Bonin Wood Pigeon, the Society Parakeet—were all hollow inside, all staged, stuffed, and dead to the world.

And at the end of the room, and at the window, the old woman watched herself in the glass and reached up and turned the metal lock on the window sash and lifted open the window, the weights in the walls banging, the night dark outside, the air cool, the sounds again of a party, the stars, the streetlamp moon. And what was so wrong with admitting it, admitting that she would love to fly home right now like a bird? That she would have given anything to go dark through the black air, instead of having to walk past the tuxedoed thickwits splashing in the fountain after the gold fish, the bare-shouldered women giggling as they held the men's shoes dry in their arms. That the insolent look of the night guard with his feet up on the desk, that look enough to crush her, those eyes enough to make her feel more small and lonely—if this made any sense at all—lonely for her life when it was as yet undiminished, for the vanishing of her life behind her.

She walked home cold under the moon—which had two blue rings around it, meaning frost—and she was home again, her red wine where she had left it on the porch, next to the chocolate and fruit. She took everything inside and sat in her chair and hugged herself with a heavy shawl wrap until her teeth stopped chattering. She stared tiredly at the room, the fireplace, the radio, the rug, her husband's empty chair, her basket of yarn. And she didn't know, in the end, how to sit without hope, how to sit without wishing for his return, for her Romeo to open his beak and place a necklace in her palm and return to her all the many voices she had grown so lonely for.

She heard the rumble of a train running through town, and then all was quiet again. She raised her palm to her mouth to taste the salt, and she heard mice in the walls. Far away a dog barked. And she must have fallen asleep, for she was awakened by the scratching in the kitchen. She feared the mice had become rats, their clawings so persistent that she took the iron poker from the fireplace with her. She turned on the light, and the noise stopped. At the counter she checked that the flour and sugar jars were closed, and when she turned to leave, the scratching like tapping began again.

Then at the back door, his hand on the screen, she caught the little gray face in the bottom corner of the screen; it was the organ grinder's monkey in his mustard-colored suit, and she smiled and let him in. "My, my," she said, "what a surprise!"

And the monkey climbed up on the counter and held out his hand to shake.

"And what brings you here, you little rascal?"

The monkey's smile widened as he went across to the table and sat down, his tail coiled around the chair back. He crossed his legs like a gentleman.

"Well, then," she said, "may I offer something to eat?"

She set the table and began putting out cheese and crackers and nuts, a tiny bowl of olives, some fruit and wine, and the monkey nibbled at a pretzel and never took his eyes from her. And when she sat down, she offered him chocolate and began her talking. She told what amounted to a long pour of days and once-upon-a-time memories, the monkey listening rapt, her voice stopping only long enough to refill a glass or crack a nut for her little friend.

Then, in the distance, they heard the voice of the organ grinder up the street. "Don't do this, Archie," he called, his voice breaking and raw. "Come home, please."

Neither the monkey nor the woman moved. They stared at one another, and the man passed the front of the house. "Arch-ie, please," he called, and neither the monkey nor the woman seemed to breathe, they held so still.

"Bad Archie," said the man. "You're a bad, mean monkey."

And when the man's voice had passed the door, the old woman stood and looked out on the street to see the organ grinder, blind and bareheaded, stumble like a drunk along the gutter in the cool moonlight. The old woman turned to Archie and watched him sleeve a butter knife, his thin brown hand taking up his glass by the stem and placing it back down in the ring of wine on the tablecloth.

"Now, Archie," she said and sat again, "where were we?"

DAVID BOTTOMS

A Morning from the Good News of John

for Reynolds Price

This morning in my bathroom mirror, I glimpsed the slope
of my shoulders, my chest thinning to a hint of ribs,
the hair of my pouching belly
black and beaded with water,
and pondering myself limp and priestly,
laced with blue veins, I judged nothing threatening.
Sometimes, I admit, I even look at this unremarkable body
which is beautiful only
in design, and feel a laughable joy.

So what is the body to be mindful of?

And I remembered the disciples who fished all night
on the sea of Tiberias
only to come in at daybreak, their boat empty.
From the shore a stranger asks what they've caught.
Nothing. Then throw to the starboard.
And there they net more fish
than they can haul. I like to think of Simon Peter
when he first catches that voice, how in one translation
he tucks up, not girds on, his shirt.
I study that moment he jumps from the boat, eyes
on the shore, hands
lifting shirt over legs, groin, hips.
I love to imagine being startled
into innocence, heedless
of the body leaping naked toward God.

Testament

Almost winter and the groundskeepers are firing
    blanks into the trees,
scattering a nuisance of grackles from the branches—
    Enough, say the guns, *enough*
of all your excrement and birdsong, and the very sight

is futility: great fistfuls
    of black confetti, the way they soar out
shrill with panic and return
    as if history would take them back, blowing
its leaves onto the trees again.

And with each return, I see a storm of words
    fall into the limbs' antennae.
They are gathering into a woman's story
    I heard on the car radio
by the lake: unforgettable: the blue

flame in the radio's face,
    that wash of occasional static in her voice.
And up ahead
    a thread of sun in the water, its light
a long thin nerve to the world.

For every profanity they put
    her through—these men who keep revisiting
her sleep—she feels profane
    to speak it, to go down that trail of burns
to the core of the disaster;

which is more than any act at the center,
    the tortuous
logic of pliers and knives, more than the open
    mouths of wounds
welling up with unspeakable life.

Beneath the scavenging aftermath of birds,
    feasting,
she knows a silence that is a parody of mercy.
    It bears a head
without a face, an inability to forgive.

She opens her mouth and birds fly out.
    They are a flock of hooks
in the sky's fabric. To remember is to be wholly herself.
    Almost dark. She opens her mouth
and the trees inhale.

KAREN BENKE

Between Words

"The space we breathe is also called distance…"
—Linda Gregg

The trail to the ocean is steep.
The grass we walk through, high and wet.
I hear clear wind sighing
through slender pine, silence
between your words:
that place your loneliness lives
where I want to slip under,
move unbroken as stone.
I know where your pulse quickens
feels like water, too deep.
I know you think you might fold into yourself,
as stars do, where words might not matter.
This place you won't go to let me hold you
is where I have gone.

Causae et Curae

You preferred to reserve a table in the corner,
and over the appetizers you may apologize,

but first we must order the cook to harvest well,
tuck away the sorry scattering of nostalgia
under a wing or beneath a bone.

No real specters this evening, as your plot
spins out over the aromas and glances off
the movie posters of gigantic love.

Your sentiments—your lost causes—are spilling over
your dinner jacket. I can't now easily interrupt
or even suggest a different meal to read you by.

Look: birds under a butter glaze. I'm a little
soothed by them imprisoned on our plates. The belief
in recipes still keeps us talking,* and you say, "Throats
of doves, crowns of peacocks," just to win me over.

If I was left to conjure, I'd rub leaves between my fingers,
add dashes and dashes, coax the smell from
the flowers' centers, and imagine how to insinuate
my misgivings with a delicate crust.

This meal you've ordered for me is in want
of a voice, a winter curtain to brush the glare away.
If only you could summon the appropriate twin fruits.

Where are the gourmets tonight? Where are they?
Your inscriptions cannot cure me, only soothe me.

---

*Place basil under your tongue if you find you can't speak.

Myopia

Yes, they were like windows, all those medical jars,
not the eyes themselves. No, they were like acorns,
or rocks, hard, solid things—enemies of glass—yet
kept safe, sealed, untouched, behind glass.

Every day I would scrutinize the jars, take them
one by one from their organized comb in the bottom
bureau drawer of my father's study. I spent hours
on the floor of that dusty room examining the vials,

each containing an eye—saved from his research
in foreign countries—left lonely, unpaired, a broken
chunk of cork trapped at the base of a bottle:
Horse, Monkey, Human, Hare...

Some were hard-skinned with a rugged layer of crust,
some floated, spun, sank in speckled bog water,
others were, as if by a mistake, perfect, the way
I pictured an eye to be—except in a jar—lolling

backwards, forwards as I tilted the glass in the C-clamp
of my fingers, watching it roll from end to end,
imagining a tonsil in the soprano's throat, rolling with
her voice rolling on the radio downstairs in the kitchen;

where my mother sang, too, balling melon for a party.
I heard them through the vents—invisible tunnels sewn into
the house; we hear each other, everywhere—could they hear
the subtle scrape, my lashes against the glass?

The thin wall separating me from a *Mink's* gauzy eye?
Perhaps the same *Mink* hanging skinned, one of how many
in the hall closet? Worn one winter night as we
stood on the walk, gawking at the accident:

black ice, sirens, a man crushed into the steering wheel,
the plush column of my mother herding us indoors...
Downstairs, that soprano soaring, her voice jumping up
the register, I'd shake the glazed orb of *Goat;* it played

like a rubber ball thudding against the glass.
With the held high note fluttering over the blender,
I removed *Infant,* whose eye was small, caked, fused
with its own rough skin to the side of the jar. Even when

turned upside down it stuck, immobile as a chrysalis:
those we gathered for school, feeling shame. No, not shame,
some reluctance, though, when the worm slid from its silver-
minted pod. We saw the rusted wings extend, watched

its first flight like a poorly made paper plane that soars,
unfolds. *Infant* eye, never used. No, perhaps used a day or two,
in what place? Hospital, taxicab, rented room with
a corner sink, blue-stained smear beneath the faucet...

I removed them all, a Stonehenge on the sun-drenched carpet.
Bowling pins, chess figures, I lay eye-level with them, focused
as the sunlight worked its way through whatever translucence
was left glossy, without patina, tunneled inside each eyeball.

Now I shut off the lights in the apartment, lie on my bed
in the streetlamp-streaked dark, scrutinizing the grid
of lit windows across the street: amorous couple overlapping
on a red couch, father strutting in his underwear, woman

hauling out her harp on Sundays an hour before
the quartet arrives, prying open their velvet-lined cases.
More interesting than violin lessons shrieking in my building,
thunder of the trash chute, snoring couple next door...

These people in their lighted cells across the street must
see me here, typing, making my bed, must have watched
me risk life and limb, leaning out to clean the glass
coated thick with grime that reveals itself in streaks when

the sun comes in to fade my blankets, bleach jackets of books,
kill the jade plant my father gave me when I moved in. Yes,
too much light—not my erratic watering, not my lack of pruning—
No, my mistake; I set it in that place to watch it grow.

DAN BELLM

Brightness

Driving home from the hospice, from his death,
four a.m. now, his last possessions in a paper bag
beside me on the seat, the heavy glasses,
the teeth in a margarine tub,
his cheap watch on my arm as though I'd stolen
time back, the smell of his skin
on my hands; over the city
where I was born there's a sliver
of glass, the new moon
with the old moon in its arms;
so dark, and no one on the streets
as if this were my dream city
that I won't have to share with anyone,
enclosed apart in its own time
but a little changed, a little decayed
from the way I remember it, separate
from me after all, going its own way; it is not
my memory; time has not stopped; my father is dead.
O ferocious soul with your famous mistrust of love,
I think your darkness
must be my inheritance;
I reach the edge of the city, drive west on Highway 36
and there is no one under the shelter of darkness
but me and two or three truckers on the road,
early risers like you, starting the working day
before anyone else has stirred; so the far past
returns and you come into my room softly
to tap me out of sleep
in the dark, we go for a ride in the truck
somewhere, you and me, shivering awake, our breath visible,
alone in our bodies,
alone in the world.

What Did You Come to See

*Jesus began to say unto the multitudes concerning John, What
went ye out into the wilderness to see? A reed shaken with the
wind? ... But what went ye out for to see? A prophet?
Yea, I say unto you, and more than a prophet.*
—Matthew 11: 7–9

There's always something sepulchral
John the Baptist wants us to see, something
that will ravish us more than he will—

see how he gestures (forerunner)
toward the timeless, sacred scene,
leading, if you follow him, the eye

away from his muscles and camel-hair rags,
hung pelts of his robe, the dark wilderness skin—
and the corrected,

redirected gaze
moves over the canvas, to the Virgin
and Corpse with arrow-

ridden, ghastly saints,
ageless, toothed
cleavers stabbed inside their haloes ...

The pointing Baptist is always there
only not to be there, to exempt
himself from the scene of redemption,

so he glares straight-on and his finger
begs us not to look at *him,*
which makes me gaze all the harder

at his honeycomb and locusts, his thin
reed cross: What did you come
to see, a reed

shaken in the wind? Icon
of not looking, of returning the gaze
to what lies far beyond the phenomenal—

So, on the highway to San Sepolcro,
road signs for miles proclaimed
PREGNANT MADONNA, NEXT EXIT—

Madonna del Parto, in her roadside shrine, restored,
but we still missed the exit, counting
whores, in gold lamé, red

leotards, waving at truckers,
while the signs
pointed, insistent: Piero

della Francesca's Madonna
del Parto, exit, exit...,
There's always something more awful

the world wants us to see, pointing
away from Christ's gestation
to the dairy truck

screeched into gravel ruts,
the prostitute's leotard split open at the crotch
as she runs to meet it, and the gaze

redirects itself, refocuses, and the sacred,
and its restored
depictions, blur...

* * *

In Palma Giovane's self-portrait,
he's so mixed in with his scene
of Transfiguration, you can hardly tell

who's the painter, who apostles and saints
with their arms cast out in astonishment
at the Christ blasted off into light:

except that he holds the splattered brush,
and so paints his own way in
even as we watch, transfiguring

his life to a scene of the holy:
how should we direct our gaze? To the painter, to Christ,
to the witnesses cowering from the blare

of light? Or look back
from what we can bear to see
to the sign of what we can't,

apostle gone blind from the sight. Icon
of unseeable splendor: what
did we come to see? A foppish

man in stole and beret, who's stared
for four hundred years, believing
his own brushstrokes could grant him entry to that
      Kingdom—

Not like the Baptist, all
beast-skin and exposed muscle, no sign
of his martyrdom, no severed head

—emplattered—to show us, who stands
ashamed of his apparition in the scene,
in a wilderness of his own making, pointing away...

I stared at his finger
crooked toward the business of the cross,
dark vein over bone in the twisted wrist,

and barely even glanced toward the Crucifixion.
Signs and wonders, wonders and signs:
it's always the diversion

that attracts me,
what doesn't mean to be seen that I need
to stare down, until it's just dried

pigment on a canvas, ground
lapis lazuli, ultramarine, daubed
strokes in eggwash and squirrel hair,

something wholly of its own time (truck stop, split
leotard) of which
it keeps telling us: Don't look.

More

More in number, five
or six at a time
perched atop stiff cat-

tail tufts or calling
from lush caverns in
the willow limbs—more

on the wing, more flash
and blood, more wild song,
who seldom travel

in numbers bigger
than a pair—the red-
wings returning this

spring to the park pond
have surprised us all.
It's supposed to be

a bad time for birds.
El Niño has scorched
California

for months, spreading east
and windward its strain
of killer drought, of

greenhouse-effect storms.
A few blocks away
the factory mill

            dusts our own fields with
a mineral mist—
pesticide spills from

            the well-water taps.
The honeybees are
dying out, and what-

            ever food the birds
are used to has thinned
next to nothing: yet

            here they are, bright as
bobbers, floating the
rich, brown surfaces.

            It's a windless day
of someone's childhood.
Small wonder so many

            of us have come
to sun with the red-
wings on the small bank.

            The birds, to see us,
must think all is well,
to see so many

            so happy to be
here . . . to see so many
more gathering now.

The Dying

When Grandma was dying
in the rope bed, no one said much.
I had pinworms, used to wake up
and hunt for them in the sheets.
Dad taught me rummy and chopsticks
on the piano. Mom took turns
with Aunt Sarah wiping Grandma
down. Mostly I wasn't allowed in
but I peeked anyhow, seeing how
she picked at her skin,
trying to pull it loose.
Last thing she said was
she was going for a cool swim.
Sarah closed the curtains,
left the ballgame on the radio
and went out to pull onion grass
in the cow pasture. Said
no one wants to taste death
and sour milk the same week.
In the night dogs woke me.
There were car lights in my window
and heat lightning.
I flicked on my light.
Mud daubers made nests
on the ceiling.
They were kind of humming.

Skiing by Moonlight

Gray cloud like a sweater pulled over the heart of the moon.
High-napped purple sky. Why are so many friends
Leaving or getting left behind?

Mao's anti-sparrow campaign: to kill and eat the birds
That were eating the grain. Winter sun drifts away
Leaving thin taffy light. Venus Mercury Jupiter—

Three pearls in the morning sky. By thinking herself
Invisible, the fox walks over hoarfrost not breaking
Morning's delicate lace. Leaving no trace. Lace is beautiful

Because of absence, the place that lets the light through,
Gives it strength. Mother Teresa in the hospital
Watches the annular eclipse. Once every twenty thousand years—

A portion of the sun visible as a ring surrounding the dark moon.
The doctor tells her—protect yourself, hold an x-ray of your lungs
Up to the window, let only the waning light pass through.

Fast trail down the mountain –10 degrees. Starving vole
Tracks ornate Victorian filigree. What is the bearing weight
Of an ice crystal? Why will a person freezing to death

Inch into the false warmth of the moon? Eros is the wound.
White will go to shadblow. White will go to orchid bloom.
Except by nature—as a woman, I will be ungovernable.

Snow Globe

It's winter in the tiny motel.
The man and woman lie down
naked and freezing. A blizzard

streaming on the television,
gloss of ice on the windows,
the bourbon a bottle of fire.

After love she licks
his cold sweat, trying to seal
herself into him.

Smoke from their cigarettes
rising, disappearing as they sink
into sleep. If I shake them

awake now they'll tumble
from the white bed,
ashes swirling and searing

their skin. Already
my hands, numb from holding them,
begin their painful prickling.

Already I'm remembering
his breath on my face, hot
as an animal's, his insistent tongue.

Better to let them
lie there, then. To let the chill
of the deep drifts bury them.

The Numbers

How many nights have I lain here like this, feverish with plans,
with fears, with the last sentence someone spoke, still trying to finish
a conversation already over? How many nights were wasted
in not sleeping, how many in sleep—I don't know
how many hungers there are, how much radiance or salt, how
     many times
the world breaks apart, disintegrates to nothing and starts up again
in the course of an ordinary hour. I don't know how God can bear
seeing everything at once: the falling bodies, the monuments and
     burnings,
the lovers pacing the floors of how many locked hearts. I want
     to close
my eyes and find a quiet field in fog, a few sheep moving toward
     a fence.
I want to count them, I want them to end. I don't want to wonder
how many people are sitting in restaurants about to close down,
which of them will wander the sidewalks all night
while the pies revolve in the refrigerated dark. How many days
are left of my life, how much does it matter if I manage to say
one true thing about it—how often have I tried, how often
failed and fallen into depression? The field is wet, each grassblade
gleaming with its own particularity, even here, so that I can't help
asking again, the white sky filling with footprints, bricks,
with mutterings over rosaries, with hands that pass over flames
before covering the eyes. I'm tired, I want to rest now.
I want to kiss the body of my lover, the one mouth, the simple
     name
without a shadow. Let me go. How many prayers
are there tonight, how many of us must stay awake and listen?

from *Falsies*

My Mother's Apogee

My mother is dressed for the occasion in a purple, lime green, and chartreuse Pucci peignoir and matching toreador pants, a latter-day transgender Joseph in her robe of many colors. I am wearing harlequin sunglasses and my father's undershirt. My sister, as yet unborn in this recurring pageant, stands by in the persona of a nurse, wearing a dishtowel that covers her hair and is pinned at the nape.

My mother lies on her back on the bed, her legs spread indecorously, and I lie between them, the top of my head tucked into the confluence of her thighs. As we do each year, we are reenacting her most satisfying achievement, a day on which she rose to her noblest and best purpose, a day compared to which all others pale.

It is an event which my mother looses from memory and replays annually before gathering it up and tucking it back in the hollow of her heart with her small hoard of joys. It is the anniversary of my birth. On this day, ten years ago, she brought me forth, living testament to a sublime moment of fusion with my father.

As if in a sealed atmosphere, like those glass snow domes that you turn upside down, bringing a tiny village to life for an instant, my mother and I and the tacit presence of my father are suspended in this finitude where no one grows old, or talks back, or is unfaithful, but remains exactly as they were on that day ten years ago before I betrayed her by growing up, a day on which she had my father's full measure of love.

My mother pretends to labor, now clutching her belly, now grunting as if bearing down, now relaxing as if between contractions. I lie in the delta of her technicolor thighs, staring at the light fixture on the ceiling. Now my mother cries out, calling into existence the newborn. This is my cue to chime in with mewling cries as I emerge from the keep of her womb.

My sister turns me over and slaps my bottom.

At last, I can breathe.

Servile

My father was a dreamer and a rainbow chaser and sometimes he took me along for the ride. My favorite times were driving in the car with him going nowhere, being nomads, him listening to some inner music, his upper lip caught in his lower teeth. It felt very restful after my mother's shrieking.

I loved watching him lean into a turn, his sleeves rolled up, his forearms bulging. I watched his hands on the steering wheel, square and capable, the fingers spatulate, worker's hands, though he was not a workman but a lawyer. The joint of his thumb, the way it stuck out as he wrapped it around the wheel, gave me comfort.

"Will you marry me when I grow up?" I asked.

"I'll be too old."

"Do you like my dress?"

"It's a nice dress."

"Do you like me better than you like Mommy?"

"That's a silly question."

"Am I pretty?"

"Shoosh. God will hear."

I took his hand from the wheel and pressed it to my lips. He left it there a moment, letting me, then he pulled it away and put it back on the wheel.

"Don't do that anymore," he said.

"Why?"

"It's servile."

"What does servile mean?"

"It means don't do it anymore."

Persian Lamb

For my mother's fortieth birthday, my father brought home two coats—a Persian lamb and a karakul—and told her to choose between them. She set the boxes on the dining room table and opened the first. When she lifted the coat from the box, the tissue paper fluttered upward like a wing. She tried it on in front of the mirror that hung over the sideboard, crossing her legs like a fashion model, even though the mirror was too high to see anything below the waist.

She looked lovely, her blond hair pulled back from her face with butterfly combs, and I sat on a chair watching her, trying to look pleased, but stewing with envy. She turned from side to side, admiring herself, and it was all I could do to keep from telling her that she looked ugly, and short, and a lot better in her cloth coat. Then she tried on the second coat, holding it close against her neck, pooching out her lips, and twirling like Loretta Young.

"Which do you like best?" she said.

In truth, I liked the karakul best because it didn't have stupid little curls, but I couldn't bear the thought of her having either of them. I was almost a teenager and it would be far more practical for me to have one.

"What's the point of getting a fur coat when you're so old? It costs a lot of money and you're going to die soon."

My mother dropped the coat on the floor, rushed at me, and smacked me in the face.

The Persian lamb was the one she ended up keeping.

One night, when she was asleep, I combed the curls out with a nit comb.

The Funeral

It is men who carry the dead in our religion, but my sister and I are adamant and my mother accedes. Stepping over hillocks of soiled snow, my sister and I walk on opposite sides of the casket, borne also by nephews and uncles. The wood digs into my fingers, cuts grooves in the pillows of my flesh. I breathe deeply, trying to sniff my father through the varnished box one last time, he who loved me too much and not enough, soon a fistful of dust. My mother wears a navy blue suit, the jacket nipped at the waist, the skirt—lined in red—slit to the thigh.

"He would have liked it," she says.

In the coffin, my father ebbs, his face gone gray as ash, those eyes I used to kiss closed like brocaded curtains, the flesh beneath them crumpled and soft. I cannot picture them without remembering his story of when he was a boy and rode half-asleep in the dark beside his father when he delivered ice on winter mornings, lulled by the rocking of the wagon wheels over the cobblestones, his hands tucked in opposite sleeves for warmth, of watching the vapor of his breath cloud before him as he shivered on the buckboard, of his father whoaing the horses, looping the tether around a post, and coming out of a customer's barn with his payment for a block of ice, two newly laid eggs still hot from the hen, which he pressed against my father's eyelids to warm him on his journey.

A Radically Condensed History
of Postindustrial Life

When they were introduced, he made a witticism, hoping to be liked. She laughed very hard, hoping to be liked. Then each drove home alone, staring straight ahead, with the very same twist to their faces.

The man who'd introduced them didn't much like either of them, though he acted as if he did, anxious as he was to preserve good relations at all times. One never knew, after all, now did one.

ABOUT STUART DYBEK

A Profile by Don Lee

Stuart Dybek works with a curious mix of spontaneity and retentiveness. He wrote most of the stories for his first collection, for instance, under a spell. He'd put on Eastern European classical music, and the words would simply pour out. To this day, Dybek relies on music for inspiration, listening to jazz, jotting in a notebook, improvising, not knowing or caring if the lines will beget a poem or a short-short or a novella. Yet he can be superstitious and fussy—a perfectionist. He is reluctant to analyze or even discuss his ongoing projects, fearing he might "talk away a story," and he has not published another book since his second collection in 1990, although he has four full-length manuscripts that have been interminably close to ready.

Dybek, a second-generation Polish American, lives in Kalamazoo, Michigan, and has taught at Western Michigan University since 1974. His wife, Caren, works in the school system near Kalamazoo, and their daughter and son were raised there. But as Dybek's readers know—and his fans are cultish in their reverence for his work—he writes almost exclusively about the Southwest Side of Chicago, where he was born in 1942. Later known as Pilsen and El Barrio, the neighborhood was populated by working-class Poles, Czechs, and Hispanics. The Catholic church bridged the various ethnic groups, which mingled with a remarkable lack of tension. "It was a benevolent time," Dybek says. The area was considered an urban ghetto, and he was in a gang, but he witnessed little oppression or violence, none of "what has become a kind of genocidal urge in lower-class neighborhoods today."

What Dybek remembers is joy. "I was an ecstatic kid," he says. He was surrounded by hundreds of children, products of the postwar baby boom, and he and his friends ran around with utter abandon, playing baseball, hopping freights, trespassing through factory grounds. His father nicknamed him "The Weed," partly because he was so skinny, mostly because he was so wild. His father, Stanley, was a foreman at the International Harvest plant,

which manufactured trucks and farm implements—including a manure spreader, regarded as "the only product we won't stand behind"—and his mother, Adeline, worked as a truck dispatcher for extra income. They were taxed enough without having to deal with their three rambunctious sons. Dybek, the oldest, attended Catholic schools throughout his childhood, and he was always getting into trouble in classes. "I was a year younger than everybody else, and because of that, I think the nuns gave me the benefit of the doubt and ascribed a lot of my behavior to immaturity, which my father knew all along should have been ascribed to weediness."

He was an indifferent student, even in college, where he was put into remedial English, but he did have his passions. A major influence was his grandmother. She barely spoke English, and Dybek hardly knew any Polish, but they had a bond that transcended language. "I was madly, madly in love with her," Dybek says. "There was just a quality of pure emotion that didn't require much in the way of language. She just made me *feel*. She had a tremendous sense of humor, and there was an ancient quality about her—odd superstitions, and body language and smells, and just everything about her communicated someplace other than

America." Another visceral, otherworldly source of emotion was music. For reasons Dybek has never been able to fathom, he became obsessed with jazz, and was determined, at eleven years old, to play an instrument. He thought of taking up the trumpet, until his brother knocked off a piece of his front tooth with a belt buckle, ruining his embouchure, so he settled on the saxophone, taking lessons and later forming a band. (They never had any professional gigs, although they occasionally joined a polka band for a couple of sets, "which was something that filled you with a certain amount of humiliation.")

Writing was a distant interest. He read quite a bit—"Again, it was in a weedlike manner"—fascinated for a time with Greek mythology, but writing itself was not imaginable as a vocation. However, Dybek does remember distinctly an epiphany that struck him in the fourth grade, when he woke up one morning to find his mother with the flu. She prepared cream of wheat for his breakfast and then went back to bed, and Dybek, who'd always hated cream of wheat, happily flushed it down the toilet and worked on a school composition about Africa. "I was trying to describe the trees in Africa, and in groping to describe how tall they were, I thought about the tallest things I'd ever seen, which were skyscrapers, and I wrote the phrase 'the tree-scraped skies.' And I mean, I had such a sudden bolt, it jacked me out of my seat at the breakfast table." He sprinted into his mother's room, where she was in the midst of vomiting. "Here she is, heaving over the side of the bed into a bucket, and here's this kid standing there reading this composition about Africa. I'd never done anything like that before. From that moment on, writing was no longer just an academic exercise."

Yet when he entered nearby Loyola University of Chicago, the first in his family to go to college, it wasn't with the intention to become a musician or a writer, but a doctor. After a year, he abandoned that folly and switched to English literature. He became heavily invested in the civil rights and antiwar movements, and his resistance to paternalistic authority, his desire for reform, led him, after graduating from Loyola in 1964, to become a caseworker for the Cook County Department of Public Aid for two years. "I think I believed that you could somehow engage in this social change, do-gooderness, with a job like that," he says.

"And one of the huge things that I learned was that, at least at that time, you were as much a part of the problem as anything else. It was a very disillusioning experience." He turned to teaching, first at an elementary school in the Chicago suburbs, then at a high school in the Virgin Islands, of all places, fulfilling a dream to be closer to the natural world (he was a closet butterfly collector as a kid—"That was the kind of thing that could get you branded for life in my neighborhood"). "One of the things that made me love teaching was that I finally did find, within the system, some kind of a job that I felt you could do with a minimum of compromises and that did have a benevolent effect on people's lives. Two of the happiest years of my life were living in the Caribbean, between being able to teach these absolutely wonderful local kids and at the same time becoming absolutely obsessed with the ocean."

Teaching would be his mission. He agreed with the philosopher John Dewey, who had deemed education to be the great democratizing force. "My goal was to reach a point where I could either do something in curriculum, or maybe even have my own school someday." But writing was now equally compelling to him, and he hoped he could do both by enrolling in the Ph.D. program at the University of Iowa, where he would be allowed to submit a creative dissertation. "I had never met a real writer at that point, and it was only after I got there, in the company of people like Richard Yates, Cheever, Don Justice, that I began to realize the enormous commitment writing really demanded." He surrendered completely to his writing, taking poetry and fiction workshops simultaneously.

His classmates—among them Tracy Kidder, T. Coraghessan Boyle, Denis Johnson, Larry Levis, Laura Jensen, Thom Jones, and Michael Ryan—challenged and inspired Dybek, but he also grew weary of the place on occasion. Dybek recalls: "I was walking across a parking lot in the rain, talking to Jon Jackson, and saying to him, 'I don't think I could stand reading another goddamn worksheet this semester'"—worksheets were how student work was distributed in those days, on mimeographs—"and suddenly, a wet piece of paper was stuck to my foot, and I pulled it off, and I said, 'Look, it's a goddamn worksheet! You can't even walk without them sticking to you.' And I looked at it, and I started reading it, and they were these fantastic poems. They were by Tom Lux. So it was that kind of place, where you'd be walking across the parking lot in the rain, and suddenly you'd be reading this wonderful stuff."

After receiving his M.F.A. in 1973, Dybek spent one year in the Florida Keys, then landed in Kalamazoo. He published a collection of poems, *Brass Knuckles* (University of Pittsburgh Press), in 1979, a collection of interrelated stories, *Childhood and Other Neighborhoods* (Viking), in 1980, and another story collection, *The Coast of Chicago* (Knopf), in 1990. Along the way, he has won a Whiting Writers' Award, a Guggenheim, an NEA fellowship, a Nelson Algren Award, numerous O. Henry Awards and *Best American Short Stories* selections, a lifetime achievement award from the American Academy of Arts and Letters, and a PEN/Malamud Award.

Dybek is one of the progenitors of the short-short as a form, and in *The Coast of Chicago*, he interleaves seven short-shorts with seven longer stories, binding them so tightly in place and theme, the book deservedly earns comparisons to Anderson's *Winesburg, Ohio,* and Joyce's *Dubliners.* In those stories, he shifts seamlessly from gritty naturalism to magic realism, transforming the tangible into the mythic. It's a metafictional technique, melding memory with imagination, that came to him listening to Eastern European music many years ago. Before then, he hadn't found a narrative voice that had suited him. He'd been trying to crank out conventional short stories with generic American characters, but they didn't feel right. Then he happened to read about the Hungarian composers Bartók and Kodály, who had toured the Hungarian countryside, seeking Gypsy music to incorporate into their own compositions. Dybek hunted down a Kodály record, and from the moment the needle hit vinyl, images of his family and his own Eastern European neighborhood appeared before him. He began reading Kafka and Isaac Babel, and started a story, "The Palatski Man," that ended up being his first publication, in *The Magazine of Fantasy and Science Fiction* (sixteen literary journals had rejected it).

Stylistically, he has become renown for his lyricism, which often borders on incantation, as evidenced in a passage from a recent story, the prize-winning "We Didn't." He takes a banal situation—a Chicago teen in the throes of hormonal delirium who cannot sway his girlfriend to sleep with him—and gives it majesty:

> Along the Gold Coast, high-rises began to glow, window added to window, against the dark. In every lighted bedroom, couples home from work were stripping off their business suits, falling to the bed, and doing it. They did it before mirrors and pressed against the glass in streaming shower stalls, they did it against walls and on the furniture in ways that required previously unimagined gymnastics which they invented on the spot. They did it in honor of man and woman, in honor of beast, in honor of God. They did it because they'd been released, because they were home free, alive, and private, because they couldn't wait any longer, couldn't wait for the appointed hour, for the right time or temperature, couldn't wait for the future, for messiahs, for peace on earth and justice for all. They did it because of the Bomb, because of pollution, because of the Four Horsemen of the Apocalypse, because extinction might be just a blink away. They did it because it was Friday night. It was Friday night and somewhere delirious music was playing —flutter-tongued flutes, muted trumpets meowing like tomcats in heat, feverish plucking and twanging, tom-toms, congas, and gongs all pounding the same pulsebeat.

Of late, Dybek's inclination to mimic the emotion of music with prose has become more explicit. "When I first started writing," he says, "I thought it would be about *saying* something. I don't think that now. I think of writing as *making* something. What's come to fascinate me more and more is trying to use language the way that the mediums of other arts—music in particular—are used, so that they lead you to nonverbal places. I don't know if it's a paradox or just foggy thinking to believe language can do the same thing, that language can in some way or another lead you to something unsayable."

His process is still to scribble in notebooks, filling pages with verse. Whether the verse eventually yields a poem or novella is somewhat unimportant, although he would like to work in longer forms more: "Genre is sometimes treated like a religion. But for me it's primarily a tool. Working in different genres, the material gets transformed in different ways." But he is careful not to rush the transformation, and faces his publisher's and his readers' demands for a new book with equanimity.

In Kalamazoo, he tends to the mail and more prosaic business in the morning, writes in the afternoon, and teaches at night, a job he continues to think of as an enormous privilege. He returns to Chicago often, visiting friends and family. He claims he doesn't need to go back to his hometown for material anymore. He has enough memories of the old neighborhood to carry him through several more books. He will, he promises, release a collection of stories and a novella soon. "I'm getting close," he insists. "That's all I can say."

ABOUT JANE HIRSHFIELD

A Profile by Peter Harris

There is a Zen saying, "Not knowing, we proceed." At some level this is true for us all. For Jane Hirshfield, such moving forward through enigma can be terrifying, but is also "the richest place to be." Having recently published a book of essays and a book of poems, she is now beginning a new collection; it's the stage she likes best, "before coherence and self-knowledge have announced themselves." When, however, her new work does announce its shape, there's little doubt it will take its inevitable-seeming place in a writing life that looks, from the outside, unusually surefooted and decisive.

Hirshfield's career might be said to have begun in first grade, when she wrote on a large sheet of lined paper: "I want to be a writer when I grow up." She had forgotten all about this youthful resolve until she published her first book of poems, whereupon her mother startled her by pulling it out of a drawer. Uncertainty aside, not many writers have had, by age six, such a clear inkling of their calling. And looking back, it seems quite right that the first book she bought, at age nine, was a collection of haiku. That attraction to things Japanese surfaced again, at Princeton, where as an undergraduate she created an independent major: creative writing and literature in translation.

If one's destiny is shaped by fateful detours, the next period in Hirshfield's life seems a particularly important swerve. Shortly after graduating from college, she won the poetry contest of *The Nation* for work written while still an undergraduate. But instead of getting an M.F.A., she decided that the best, perhaps the only, way for her to move forward was to study Zen. A few months were enough to teach her how little she knew, and after a year, she made the decision to enter monastic practice, during which time she knew she'd stop writing poetry altogether. "I had to be willing to walk away from poetry, perhaps forever, before I felt like I could do it at all." What began as a month's commitment turned into eight years of study with the San Francisco Zen Center, including three years at Tassajara, living in deep wilderness with-out electricity—quite a change for someone born in Manhattan, in 1953, and raised on the Lower East Side.

After leaving formal Zen training, Hirshfield wrote two books of poetry, *Alaya* in the *Quarterly Review of Literature* series (1982) and *Of Gravity & Angels* from Wesleyan (1988). And she returned to the work, begun as an undergraduate, of translating Japanese women's poetry. With Mariko Aratani, she published *The Ink Dark Moon: Love Poems by Ono no Komachi and Izumi Skikibu* (Scribners, 1988; Vintage Classics, 1990). They are luminous English versions of two woman poets from ninth- and tenth-century Japan, a golden age for poetry, and the only one in which, Hirsh-field says, "women writers were the predominant geniuses." More recently she has published, to considerable acclaim, two more collections: *The October Palace* (1994) and *The Lives of the Heart* (1997), both from HarperCollins.

To support herself as a poet, she has evolved what she calls a "tripod" of vocations: teacher, reader, and editor. Although she has chosen not to permanently institutionalize herself, Hirshfield has been a visiting poet at various universities, mostly recently Berkeley, and serves regularly on the staff of several writers' con-ferences. Because her poetry is pellucid and speaks directly to the heart, it is not surprising that readings, from Maine to California, have given her a second means of sustenance. Third, and not least, Hirshfield has a distinguished record of translation and editing. After *The Ink Dark Moon* had whetted her taste for recoveries of women's poetry, she gathered, and often created new English versions of, poems by sixty-six different figures, from ancient Sumeria to modern Korea, published as *Women in Praise of the Sacred: 43 Centuries of Spiritual Poetry by Women* (HarperCollins, 1994). Moreover, she was deeply involved as an editor for three very successful spiritual guidebooks, Jack Kornfield's *A Path with Heart* and Thomas Moore's *Care of the Soul* and *Soul Mates*.

The range of things to which she turns her mindfulness re-minds one of a short poem she co-translates in *Women in Praise of the Sacred*. It is by Chiyo-ni, an eighteenth-century Buddhist: "From the mind / of a single, long vine, / one hundred opening lives." One of the most refreshing elements of Hirshfield's long

Jerry Bauer

vine is that its blossoms are colored by an astonishing variety of sources. Like many of her contemporaries, she writes free verse in American diction, and she loves Whitman, Dickinson, Kinnell, Bishop, Snyder, and Hass—not to mention those other "American" influences, Neruda, Rilke, Milosz—but it is her acquaintance with profoundly exotic sensibilities—from India, China, and especially Japan—that lend her work a distinct depth and air. Her recent book of essays on poetry, *Nine Gates: Entering the Mind of Poetry,* does for poetry what Pound intended to do at the turn of the century: through juxtaposition of the familiar and the unknown, it reinvigorates our thinking about the possibilities of the art. One difference is that Hirshfield's remarks are more fully considered. Twelve years in gestation, two years in the writing, *Nine Gates* is surely one of the most eloquent books ever written about poetry. And even if it weren't, the range of its apposite allusions would set it apart. For example, in the essay "Poetry and the Mind of Indirection," there are references we might expect to Joyce, Hass, Zbigniew Herbert, but they are made vivid and fresh in part because they are weighed in the same balance as allusions to Izumi Shikibu, Bashō, and Chuang-tzu.

As to Hirshfield's own poetry and its influences, anyone with more than a passing acquaintance with Zen Buddhism can feel, and savor, its organic incorporation into her work. Thematically, for instance, the emphases on compassion, on the preexistent unity of subject and object, on nature, on the self-sufficient suchness of being, on the daunting challenge of accepting transitoriness—all are central to Buddhism. Of course, every American poet after Pound and Williams owes a debt to the image-centered poetics of Japanese and Chinese verse. Hirshfield herself resists, rightly, being labeled a "Buddhist poet." Unlike, say, Gary Snyder, who consciously foregrounds Zen, she makes only a few allusions in her work to the literature of Zen. One of the attractions for her of Zen monasticism was that the stage of sequestered, intensive study is designed to come to an end. Just as Zen itself merges with the ordinary, its students reenter the world. At a certain point in one's practice, Hirshfield says, "there is no Zen, only life." Thus, the path she has chosen for herself is the one least obviously Buddhist; it is called, in Japan, "teahouse practice." In this analogy, there is a teahouse, run by an old lady who is quietly wise in the dharma, alongside a dusty road. "Nobody," Hirshfield says, "knows why they like to go in there to get their tea. But they do. That kind of unobtrusive awareness is what I want to bring to my poems." The Zen is not obviously apparent, but she assumes "it gets in the tea somehow."

Hirshfield has faith that "everything" gets in the tea somehow. She finds numinosity in the words "wholeness" and "interconnectedness." Hirshfield sees all imaginative writers, even apparently ego-centered ones, even Norman Mailer, as liminal or threshold characters, with boundary-crossing proclivities. Writers in the act of writing become permeable to the world. "When novelists describe a room," she says, "they are speaking for the paint, for the window, for the couch, for reality. Even though self is where style resides, at the moment you are writing, the self becomes transparent or translucent."

Unusual as it may sound to say that a writer speaks for paint, it is a proposition entirely consistent with Hirshfield's outlook: in fact, we cannot avoid the pigmentation of the world. "We are continuous with everything around us." Wholeness, in her view, is not just an aesthetic category or a psychological state, implying integration. Wholeness is our intrinsic condition, the condition of the world. "Poetry's job," she says, "is to discover wholeness and create wholeness, including the wholeness of the fragmentary and the broken." In Hirshfield's poems, one of the happy corollaries of accepting the unified manifold of experience is the impression they give of serenity, of radiance. For example, while stuck inside on a rainy day, the speaker in "Percolation," a poem included in *The October Palace,* meditates herself beyond stuckness into the conviction that:

> Surely all Being at bottom is happy:
> soaked to the bone, sopped at the root,
> fenny, seeped through, yielding as coffee grounds
> yield to their percolation, blushing, completely seduced,
> assenting as they give in to the downrushing water,
> the murmur of falling, the fluvial, purling wash
> of all the ways matter loves matter—

But just because the world, in an absolute sense, soaks us does not mean it is easy to accept a condition that may feel like drownedness. On the contrary, for Hirshfield such acceptance presents a profound challenge. She says Zen does not end suffering: "It hasn't made me immune to anything. Life, for me, continues to feel tremendously hard." Good literature, she feels, verges on a dark precipice. The job of poetry "is not to shine a light which causes darkness to diminish or vanish; it is to bring even darkness into visibility. My poems are not just affirmations, but what I hope are visibly hard-won affirmations. Affirmations that don't negate the despair out of which they very often come." An example might be the opening of "Mule Heart" from *The Lives of the Heart:*

> On the days when the rest
> have failed you,
> let this much be yours—
> flies, dust, an unnameable odor,
> the two waiting baskets:
> one for the lemons and passion,
> the other for all you have lost.

When asked about the respective roles of nature and politics in her poetry, Hirshfield characteristically sees the two realms as related. Or rather, she proffers, then erases, a distinction between the natural and what she has called the "chronicled world": "One of the marks of being human is that we reside amidst all of the stories that we have created to examine our existence more thoroughly—scientific, political, historical, psychological, mythic. At the same time we exist in a continuum with non-human being." One of the effects of Zen training has been to de-center her inherited Western worldview. "I am actually not all that human-centered. I know that many, many people would disagree with this stance. Both the Judeo-Christian and the Marxist worlds would disagree." But for her, the natural and political are, in an absolute sense, not distinct. "If you exploit nature you will exploit people. If you find somehow at the most fundamental level of being that your relationship to other people, other things, other animals, is a relationship of kinship then you perhaps will behave ethically in the world." Because she dwells with this radical vision of kinship, her poems are only infrequently political, but hearteningly compassionate. Like Milosz, whom she sees as the greatest living poet, she refrains from accusations. Perhaps the closest she comes is "The Ritual," in *The October Palace,* a response to Tiananmen Square. She begins indirectly by considering the fate of Wu Feng, two centuries removed. An emissary from China to Formosa, Wu Feng lived with the Formosan mountain tribes, but was troubled by their rituals of human sacrifice. Unable to persuade them to stop, he disguised himself, offered himself as a victim, and was sacrificed. This supreme act of compassion shocked and shamed the elders into stopping the practice. Only after presenting us with the case of Wu Feng does Hirshfield turn in "The Ritual" to the events of our own time. She ends the poem with three questions:

> Did the student-scholars know of him,
> the ones who, so much younger, gave the same?
> Did they use chops like his to sign their names,
> an equally brilliant Chinese red surrounding the carved-out absence?
> And the elders, these new elders—what of them?

The question, which hangs eloquently in the silence at the end of the poem, leaves open the possibility that the new elders may be unshameable. Hirshfield leaves us with a yang-yin image: a bright red signature emblematic of sacrifice, inside of which is a carved-out absence that includes the elders. But if, as she believes, "we are continuous with everything," has Hirshfield not reminded us that we are all part of both the circular signature and the emptiness inside?

Peter Harris is the director of the creative writing program at Colby College in Waterville, Maine. He is the author of a book of poems, Blue Hallelujahs, *and he has written the "Poetry Chronicle" column for* The Virginia Quarterly Review *for the past decade.*

A FOUR-SIDED BED *A novel by Elizabeth Searle. Graywolf Press,* $14.95 *paper. Reviewed by Fred Leebron.*

In her first novel, *A Four-Sided Bed,* Elizabeth Searle, the 1992 winner of the Iowa Short Fiction Award, ambitiously tackles the shifting boundaries of love and sexuality. Over the course of a telling year, two men and two women struggle to define their relationships with each other in the face of AIDS, pregnancy, and complications wrung from a present that has become decisively disconnected from its unnervingly emotional and essential past.

Allie has married the mysterious Jimmy Joe, or JJ, a librarian at the college she attends who earlier was confined to a mental institution. On the brink of pregnancy, Allie begins to intercept letters involving two of JJ's ex-fellow patients, Kin Hwang and Bird. Gradually Allie comes to realize that Kin is a man, Bird a woman, and that the man she thought she knew as her husband is in fact the third side to a passionate and in some sense everlasting bisexual love triangle.

In the novel's first half, these truths emerge via the letters Bird sends to JJ—letters which Allie at first keeps from him. Bird's voice arises as compressed and lyrical, rhythmic and evocative; her letters possess an undeniable purity. "Trapped, Kin said last night," writes Bird. "And I remembered gnawing my wood crib bars. Mother worked days, serving drinks. I chewed black nylons she left draped on my crib. She'd peel off that silky electric skin in our cold room, static crackling."

Into the second half of *A Four-Sided Bed,* Allie's elaborate strategies to keep her husband from his former lovers erode, and JJ slips across the border into Mexico to confront the AIDS-stricken Kin and his "wife" Bird in a frank and sultry scene that is wrought with sensitivity and grace. "The State of Not-Self," the dying Kin says to JJ. "I only know one way to reach any such state, Jimmy Joe. Remember? We used to call it going, not coming. All your desires, even your body itself. Just...gone." And finally, all barriers in the narrative crack as JJ returns from Mexico with Kin and Bird, both to save them and to offer his wife the fundamental truth that he has been so long and so careful in hiding.

Given the dual narrative and the forcefully suggested subtext of Bird's early letters, some readers may grow impatient with Allie's chase to comprehend the facts of JJ's relationship with Bird and Kin. But it's precisely her persistent and urgent struggle to understand, as the critical elements of her current life shift dangerously underfoot, that makes A Four-Sided Bed such an honest and resonant novel.

Fred Leebron is the author of the novel Out West *and the co-editor of the anthology* Postmodern American Fiction. *He teaches at Gettysburg College.*

WE LIVE IN BODIES *Poems by Ellen Doré Watson. Alice James Books, $9.95 paper. Reviewed by Marcus Cafagña.*

Ellen Doré Watson writes a poetry of elegy. The poems in her first book, *We Live in Bodies,* seek consolation for all the losses that diminish the human body, the loss of life, the trauma of violence, even the slow degeneration brought on by age. With dazzling turns of phrase, her poems embody a speaker who, caught in the convulsive futility of grief, attempts to preserve at least the memory of what she's lost, in this case, a miscarried fetus: "after you became a matter of blessed fact, a euphoric / knot of nausea I sat hugging, grinning my goofy / *we beat the odds grin*—to have you dead in there."

Like Larry Rivers with his painting for the book's cover, *Me in a Rectangle,* Watson both laments and celebrates the spirit housed in the body, trapped within walls, or made manifest by shape and form. With an unabashed sense of verve and humor ("Love— even forbidden love—doesn't deserve linoleum"), these poems struggle against the lassitude and consequence of loss and refuse to accept age-old misrepresentations of the body. "Tenderness rarely appears," her poem "What Gets Left Out of History Books" begins, "People don't sigh. There's no burping." The poem's meditation on starving children belies the complex metaphysical revelation beneath its surface: "The children in these pages wear distended bellies or tiny / crowns; they sing under a spotlight or lie in mass graves. / Where are the peach trees, the pies? Where are you and I?"

Watson's elegiac verse is frequently composed in the second-person, her apostrophes most affecting when addressed to a former lover, "if you could know and believe / that while they wired and shocked you I was home breathing in / your blue work-shirt, that my needing your smell on my skin / contained more electricity"; a child dying in an ambulance, "We sweep wind into her mouth / and her lips pink up. This allows us / to pretend she is alive"; or the battered toddler to whom she offers this advice: "Best to forgive them now, / before it gets worse; / that way you'll have some / forgiveness left for later."

Her unrelenting wit eschews theatrical posturing, so that lines like "If they beat all the life / out of you" consistently transcend their painful focus into "red dragonflies with wings half air, / half spun gold, gazillions of them," and culminate in courageous and unexpected conclusions, so that cruel parental hands which pummel the toddler's body "will rise up / and bear you to the warm basket waiting / beside the stove of God. Well. Whatever death / turns out to be, it will be one good mother." These elegies address not only those who are dead or absent, but extol an acceptance, for all its vagaries, of the body as "the walk-in vanity, / the basementful of self-disgust. As old as peekaboo: I loves me, / I loves me not."

In the tradition of Walt Whitman's "I Sing the Body Electric" and the nineteenth-century physiological movement that called for the candid recognition of both male and female bodily functions, Watson—like the Brazilian poet Adélia Prado, whom she has translated—sounds this timeless affirmation. "We live in bodies clumsy and disobedient," the book's title poem declares, "and we love them even as we punish with too much or too little." In poem after poem in *We Live in Bodies,* "words hover fleshless in vowels and consonants" and, despite the persistence of bodily loss and suffering, bid us to drink from the "cup of having to go on."

Marcus Cafagña's book, The Broken World, *was selected for the National Poetry Series and published in 1996 by the University of Illinois. He has poems forthcoming in* Boulevard, DoubleTake, *and* The Southern Review.

MY SISTER LIFE *A memoir by Maria Flook. Pantheon Books, $25.00 cloth. Reviewed by Kathryn Rhett.*

The author of the novels *Open Water* and *Family Night,* Maria Flook turns to memoir in *My Sister Life: The Story of My Sister's*

Disappearance, and delivers an original, gripping, intensely moving story. In 1964, Flook's fourteen-year-old sister Karen disappears, never to return home. Flook, at twelve, is left behind as the only child, but she continues to feel twinned to Karen: "I recognized a mysterious 'sister life' unfolding parallel to mine."

The break between childhood and adolescence can be traumatic, and in *My Sister Life,* it is as cataclysmic as the sinking of a ship, one of the book's leitmotifs. The sinking of the ocean liner *Andrea Doria* in 1956 haunts Flook, for in fact her family had tickets for that very passage, but changed their plans at the last minute. Maria and Karen would have been in stateroom 52. Ironically, two other sisters took their place in the room, and when the *Doria* collided with the *Stockholm,* they were separated forever, one killed, the other pulled from the wreckage.

The attempt to resurrect a lost sisterhood, through language, feels as mammoth an undertaking as restoring the *Doria* to its luminous perfection. Boldly, Flook chooses to imagine her sister's life and present it, in the first-person, through Karen's point of view: "Karen walks ahead of me through these pages. She's holding a shoe box of scraps, notes with her half of the story. I am writing this down as it happens." What happens is awful—Karen becomes a prisoner of fifty-year-old James in a trailer home, then a naval base prostitute—but we are not allowed to stop looking. "Four days after we arrived in Virginia Beach, he burns my clothes. He tells me not to answer the telephone."

As children, Flook's parents didn't have it easy, either. Her father, Ray, was sent to an orphanage by his mother after his father died. Her mother, Veronica, was locked in an apartment alone every night while her French immigrant parents presided over their restaurant. But as parents, Veronica and Ray are shocking, she for her coldness, he for his passive complicity in the rejection of their children. The couple, Flook tries to explain, "were under the spell of an intense erotic sorcery." Described as a sultry Vivien Leigh, Veronica (never called Mother here) flirts, vamps, and plots her children's early departures from home. If Flook has come from a legacy of abandonment, *My Sister Life* is her attempt to reclaim, to hold fast, to say passionately throughout her own first-person chapters, "Karen and I were *one.*"

Karen and Maria's lives converge at alarming points: they both run away, get locked in rooms by sexual partners, go to jail, and even check into the same hospitals, once on the same day. Sometimes the convergence feels expressive of individual need, Maria pursuing connection with Karen, or Flook, as a writer, constructing parallel biographies. Ultimately, convergence feels like doom, that their parents have set them on a cruel and self-destructive course. One daughter runs away, one stays home, and they both suffer. Who made the better decision? Or is life's journey a matter of fate, inevitability, like their chance escape from the *Andrea Doria*?

Flook's style is a decisive attempt to embrace the world in all of its grotesquerie and beauty. Unlike her superficial mother, Maria the girl insists on seeing everything—searching, for example, for invisible trails of rat urine at her riding stable through ultraviolet goggles. Flook the writer insists on including spider guts and glistening phalluses, along with beach roses and the Mediterranean. Inclusiveness applies to mood and pacing as well. There is mortal seriousness here, and humor, and intense drama, and meditation. There are stunning singular actions and recurrent images. There is everything a reader could want from an invented world, and such a satisfying book is rare. The well-wrought language shows us elusive truths without showing off. Flook has found a way to give all of her gifts in this book. Can two narrative voices create the whole story? The answer in *My Sister Life* is yes, and the book triumphs as a fully realized enactment of desire.

Kathryn Rhett is the author of Near Breathing, *a memoir, and the editor of the anthology* Survival Stories.

DARK SKY QUESTION *Poems by Larissa Szporluk. Beacon Press, $12.00 paper. Reviewed by Susan Conley.*

In Larissa Szporluk's startling first collection of poems, *Dark Sky Question*, winner of the 1997 Barnard New Women Poets Prize, one finds a fiercely independent voice mapping the geography of longing. Here the backdrop of a darkening sky is just one small mystery in an entire universe that poses itself as unknowable: "a warm place at the end / / of a grove of horned trees..." ("Krell"). The book unfolds as a search to uncover answers, yet nothing is conventional or linear about Szporluk's investigation.

Szporluk probes the realm of religion, but not the religion of prayer and salvation to which we have become accustomed. It is a much more irrational notion of God she writes about, with bold, open-hearted intensity. There is a kind of monasticism at work, an austerity to the brilliant descriptions, but also a deep willingness to plumb the depths. The language is subtle; it doesn't once raise its voice, issuing instead quiet, solemn directives: "leave if you're leaving. Leave plain mud."

Szporluk weaves a subversive undertone between the lines which disrupts any notion of traditional autobiography. We find a fierce self-examination here, but without much of the narcissism inherent in a great deal of American poetry. In her poems, we see traces of the tight, experimental, interior tradition of Emily Dickinson or Lorraine Niedecker, or perhaps Fanny Howe: "I don't pray. / I just walk out there / where it's thin / with my bow and aim." She creates a whole new lexicon with which to speak of absence and desire, and language for her is more significant than that which it signifies: "A man says 'the best thing here is the moon,' he feels happier than if he'd seen it." Yet Szporluk also understands how consistently language will let us down, how it will lie, how language will even fail God: "He arrives and looks around, and doesn't know the word for wind, and wind is the subject..." ("Krell").

The poems here are quirky, rigorous, and demanding. The line breaks and stanzas move quickly and decisively. They sustain themselves on their own edginess and originality rather than plot or narrative, and challenge the reader within their tight confines: "There was no moon, only space / in the waves, like a vow unmade, / or a cage whose interior flew..." ("Secrets of Jove").

The speaker of many of these poems, grappling with marriage and motherhood, is deeply wary of domestication, of obscuring her vision by way of routine. In "Occupant of the House," the voice is cool and clinical and slightly resentful: "Like a pure wild race / captured for science, too wronged / to go back, too strange to be damaged, / my fierceness has disappeared. / If it doesn't end soon, the pain will dilute, / the sin turn to sheen in the garden, / your routine a genial rain... / I wouldn't know about my body..."

These poems don't pretend to believe in redemption, yet at times they are nostalgic for the old order: "why can't eternity be where they were, back in the chain, the pull for the worm, scrape

with the carnivore, the feeling of constant attraction forever..."
("Biology of Heaven"). Szporluk demands more than "this airy
regularity. / Not this luminous branchlessness. / There is nothing
to study. / The anxiety reaches a pitch... / One lone voice chokes
on its obstinance— / *I'm human, I'm human, I know that I know.*"

Dark Sky Question is enormously successful poetry for an
unpredictable universe. Szporluk has written poems that cleave to
language and reinvent the workings of the mind, but most impor-
tantly, poems that are also fiercely attached to the workings of the
heart.

Books Recommended by
Our Advisory Editors

Mary Gordon recommends *Defiance,* a novel by Carole Maso: "A wholly original, darkly brilliant, and poetic novel about a mathematician who murders her students." (Dutton)

Fanny Howe recommends *I Love Dick,* a first novel by Chris Kraus: "A highly charged description of an obsession with an indifferent man named Dick, this unfolds as a brilliant intertextual document—feminist and contemporary in all its anxieties and passions. Important!" (Semiotexte)

Maxine Kumin recommends *When the Fighting Is All Over,* a memoir by Katie Letcher Lyle: "Katie Letcher remet her father, a Marine Corps World War II hero, when she was eight years old. He had been gone for more than four years, and neither of them was the same when he returned. Her memoir is an appealing, sensitive, poignant, yet totally unsentimental portrait of an authoritarian parent, a man given to huge rages. The complexity of her love-hate relationship with him over his long lifetime—he lived to the age of ninety-one—is familiar, yet fresh and surprising. But the book is much more than one person's story; it critiques the American Dream and adds immensely to our sense of the history of the era." (Longstreet)

Joyce Peseroff recommends *An Ark of Sorts,* poems by Celia Gilbert: "A powerful, beautifully written book with a compelling subject. In this delicately shaped series of poems, a mother recalls the passage of a year after the death of a child. An apartment in Paris is first a place of exile, then a place of refuge as the poet, with her family, mourns. Each detail in these vivid poems takes us farther and more poignantly into the city the poems describe and into the place in the heart where the poet lives. ' "The art," says Mademoiselle / "lies in the way you get / from one note to the other," ' Gilbert writes in 'The Secret'; *An Ark of Sorts* evinces that art throughout its sequence of clear images and carefully delineated feeling." (Alice James)

New Books by
Our Advisory Editors

Russell Banks, *Cloudsplitter,* a novel: About one of the most controversial figures in American history, the abolitionist John Brown, Banks's epic novel is narrated by Brown's son and comrade, Owen. The novel not only traces Brown's crusade against slavery, leading to his famous raid on Harpers Ferry in 1859, but also becomes a deeply moving portrait of an American family. (HarperCollins)

Mary Gordon, *Spending,* a novel: Gordon explores new territory with an indelibly vibrant, witty character, Monica Szabo, a fifty-year-old artist who decides to accept a handsome commodities trader as her patron. He gives her money, sex, and poses as a model. However, when her new series of paintings makes her rich, famous, and controversial, her patron has a reversal of fortune, and she must face the moral questions about art, money, and love that she has chosen, up to now, to delay answering. (Scribner)

Donald Hall, *Without*, poems: In his fourteenth collection, Hall writes with grief, grace, and courage about the poet Jane Kenyon, his late wife. The first half sketches her illness and death. The second half is comprised of verse letters he addresses to Kenyon in the ensuing year. This book stands as a poignant and powerful testimony to both love and loss, celebration and lament. (Houghton Mifflin)

Fanny Howe, *Nod*, a novel, illustrated by Inger Johanne Grytting: Howe's bravura new book defies category, presenting a fable in prose, verse, and woodcuts. About two Irish-German-American sisters in Dublin just as World War II is about to begin, the story's subtext is far-reaching and mythic, as eighteen-year-old Irene falls for her mother's ex-lover, separating her even further from her sister, Cloda. (Sun & Moon)

James Alan McPherson, *Crabcakes*, a memoir: McPherson's first new book since his 1978 story collection *Elbow Room*, which won the Pulitzer Prize, *Crabcakes* artfully describes his departure from his beloved Baltimore in the late seventies to Iowa City, where he continues to teach. The second half of the book recounts his recent trips to Japan, where he found renewal and acceptance. This beautiful book resonates as a personal meditation on race, self, and community. (Simon & Schuster)

Gary Soto, *Junior College*, poems: Soto's new collection is a touching and often hilarious account of his coming of age in Fresno, California, where he was a terrible student, graduating from high school with a D average, then attending Fresno City College with the "easiest of majors," geography. As always, Soto's memories of his Chicano family, friends, and neighborhood appeal universally with seductive language and storytelling. (Chronicle)

Maura Stanton, *Life Among the Trolls*, poems: The cool, elegant surfaces of the narratives and lyrics in Stanton's third collection conceal fiery depths. She penetrates the disguises which cloak the Iago-like figures—friends, bosses, lovers, colleagues—who manipulate our world, and who would like to remake us in their image. (Carnegie-Mellon)

Gerald Stern, *This Time: New and Selected Poems:* In his tenth book, Stern collects many poems, from 1972–1995, that are no longer available in other editions. Those favorite works, along with new poems, including affecting elegies to Larry Levis and Allen Ginsberg, prove why Stern is regarded as one of our masters, a modern Walt Whitman. (Norton)

Derek Walcott, *The Bounty*, poems: The 1992 Nobel Prize winner lovingly evokes his native land, the island of St. Lucia, in this luminous new book. Haunting, magnificent, *The Bounty* gives us Walcott at the top of his form. (Noonday)

Miscellaneous Notes · Spring 1998

JOHNNY APPLESEED When Andrew Carroll was a junior at Columbia University, a friend gave him a copy of a speech by Joseph Brodsky. Carroll was studying English literature at the time, but he had chosen the major for purely utilitarian reasons— his ambition was to become a movie and television producer, and he had heard that a well-rounded humanities background would help toward that end. He was not a poetry aficionado, and he did not know who Brodsky was. "My best guess was that he was a cosmonaut," Carroll recalls. "The name was vaguely familiar, and I was thinking, Russian, he's either a famous chess player or a cosmonaut." But the speech by the Nobel Prize winner and U.S. Poet Laureate ended up changing Carroll's life.

Arnold Browne

Brodsky declaimed that poetry should be available everywhere, that "an anthology of American poetry should be found in the drawer in every room in every motel of the land." Carroll was moved to write to Brodsky, who, much to Carroll's surprise, replied, suggesting they meet. For the next year or so, they rendezvoused at Maurizio's Café in Greenwich Village and hatched a plan. In 1993, they created a not-for-profit organization called the American Poetry & Literacy (APL) Project, and they approached hotels and publishers, hoping to realize their dream of placing poetry books next to Gideon Bibles. The initial reaction was less than enthusiastic. One hotel manager said, "Who's this Robert Frost you work for?" But then Doubletree Hotels consented, and the Book-of-the-Month Club agreed to donate an astounding ten thousand copies of the anthology *Six American Poets*.

The project has flourished since then, distributing over 125,000 free books of poetry in various cities and locales, ranging far beyond the drawers of hotel rooms to Amtrak trains, airports, homeless shelters, and vehicle inspection stations. The reception has been overwhelmingly positive, although occasionally people are wary about accepting a book from a stranger. "They often think, This is some sort of weird cult, isn't it?" Carroll reports. "But once they know there're no strings attached, they'll ask for more copies." Word has spread, and the APL Project has been inundated with requests for copies, particularly from schools and literacy centers. "It's just exploded," Carroll says. "We can't keep up with the demand." Brodsky died of a heart attack in 1996, but Carroll has carried on as the organization's executive director in Washington, D.C., with a handful of volunteers. He has been a tireless missionary, not even receiving a salary until last July, when a grant from the Gladys Krieble Delmas Foundation made a stipend possible.

As we go to press, Carroll, who is now twenty-eight, is preparing for his most ambitious project to date: to drive from New York to San Francisco in April, handing out 100,000 free books of poetry along the way. Coordinated by the Academy of American Poets during the third annual National Poetry Month, the trip is being called the Great APLseed Giveaway, and lists the Washington State Apple Growers among its funders. In his donated Ryder truck, Carroll will stop at supermarkets, jury waiting rooms, libraries, late-night diners, prisons, and shopping malls, giving away Dover Publications editions of *101 Great American Poems* and *African-American Poetry,* as well as other anthologies. Carroll is a bit apprehensive about the cross-country tour, since he has never driven more than four hundred miles at a stretch, and he did flunk his driving test three times as a sixteen-year-old. But he relishes this opportunity to go out into the field, gathering new ideas about how to make poetry a part of everyday life. One suggestion, for instance, recently came out of the blue: Why not print poems in the phone book? "My God," Carroll reflects, "we'd been saying for years that we want to make poetry as ubiquitous as phone books, and we'd never put the two of them together." He contacted a few phone-book publishers, and now, in some Yellow Pages, there is Robert Frost's "The Road Not Taken" under the heading *Travel,* and Emily Dickinson's "I Died for Beauty" under *Insurance.*

Some have questioned why the APL Project concentrates so much on the standard canon and on not contemporary poetry, and also have asked if poetry in general—considering its putative difficulty—can be effective as a literacy tool. "What's so extraordinary about classic American poetry is its disarming simplicity," Carroll explains. "It's very accessible for people of different backgrounds and reading levels. And actually that kind of poetry, with its rhyme and meter, is the best way to be introduced to language. People can get into the music of the words, even though they may not fully understand them. That's why poetry resonates, because there is a depth to it. Everyone finds something different in poetry—solace, inspiration, catharsis. But for me, the greatest thing about poetry is that we live in this incredibly fast-paced technological society, and poetry forces us to slow down and focus on what's meaningful—passion, and craftsmanship, whimsy, imagination, creativity, humanity."

Carroll has also edited an anthology, *Letters of a Nation: A Collection of Extraordinary American Letters* (Kodansha), the proceeds for which support the APL Project. The book contains over two hundred epistles, from 1630 to 1996, by the famous and the obscure. It took Carroll over six years to accumulate them all, inspired after his family home burned down and he lost his own letters. The work was difficult, especially since he is not an historian: "I have this odd tendency of picking projects I don't know much about and then immersing myself in them. But there is a connection between letters and poems. They're probably the two most egalitarian art forms we have. Anyone with a piece of paper and a pen can sit down and create a masterpiece."

With his seemingly boundless energy, Carroll is pursuing many plans for the future. He would like to raise enough money to distribute a total of one million poetry books by the millennium, put a book in every hotel and motel room in Salt Lake City during the 2002 Winter Olympic Games, and get an astronaut to read poems on the Space Shuttle. Sometime or another, Carroll's full-time participation with the project will end, as he wants to teach high school English, but he will ensure that the endeavor continues: "I can't begin to tell you how great it is to give out free books to people, books that will have a real impact."

ONE SIDE OF THE RIVER Poets Kurt Brown and Emily Hiestand and audio producer Peter Dunn have released a two-CD collection of readings by thirty-six poets from Cambridge and Somerville,

Massachusetts, called *One Side of the River* (Say That! Productions). Over half of the poets have been published in *Ploughshares,* an impressive list including Frank Bidart, Lucie Brock-Broido, Marie Howe, Gail Mazur, Robert Pinksy, Liam Rector, David Rivard, and Lloyd Schwartz.

This might be a new, homespun venture, but the quality of the performances and the acoustics are exquisite and undeniably professional. Kurt Brown says that more CDs are in the offing, with poets from the other side of the river, Boston, as well as New York City. Right now, *One Side of the River* is available only in Harvard Square bookstores, but distribution arrangements are evolving. Those outside the area may order the CD collection through the Grolier Book Shop, 6 Plympton St., Cambridge, MA 02138. The telephone numbers are (617) 547-4648 and (800) 234-POEM; the fax number is (617) 547-4230. Retail price: $29.95, plus $4 for UPS shipping. Massachusetts residents should add $1.50 for tax. The Grolier accepts all major credit cards.

CONTRIBUTORS' NOTES

Spring 1998

KIM ADDONIZIO has two volumes of poetry from BOA Editions, *The Philosopher's Club* and *Jimmy & Rita*. She is the co-author, with Dorianne Laux, of *The Poet's Companion: A Guide to the Pleasures of Writing Poetry* (Norton). She lives in San Francisco.

SANDRA ALCOSSER's second collection of poems, *Except by Nature*, was chosen by Eamon Grennan for the 1997 National Poetry Series and is forthcoming from Graywolf Press. Her first book, *A Fish to Feed All Hunger*, was an AWP Award Series winner, selected by James Tate. A livre d'artistes, *Sleeping Inside the Glacier*, was recently published by Brighton Press. She lives in Montana and teaches in the graduate writing program at San Diego State University.

NIN ANDREWS is the author of *The Book of Orgasms*. Her poems have been published in literary magazines and anthologies such as *The Paris Review, The Virginia Quarterly, Michigan Quarterly Review,* and *The Best American Poetry 1997*.

DAVID BAKER's new book of poems, *The Truth About Small Towns*, will be published this summer by the University of Arkansas Press. Poems are forthcoming in *The Yale Review, Raritan, Poetry,* and *The Virginia Quarterly Review*. He serves as a poetry editor of *The Kenyon Review* and teaches at Denison University.

BRUCE BEASLEY's collection of poems, *Summer Mystagogia*, was selected by Charles Wright for the 1996 Colorado Prize. He also won the 1993 Ohio State University Press/Journal Award for *The Creation*. He teaches at Western Washington University.

DAN BELLM's collection of poems, *Buried Treasure*, won the 1995 Alice Fay DiCastagnola Award of the Poetry Society of America. His work has appeared in *Poetry, The Threepenny Review, TriQuarterly,* and *The Village Voice*. The recipient of a 1997–98 poetry fellowship from the California Arts Council, he lives in San Francisco.

NATHANIEL BELLOWS lives in New York City. He has work forthcoming in *Western Humanities Review* and *The Paris Review*.

MOLLY BENDALL's collection of poems, *After Estrangement*, was a winner in the Peregrine Smith Poetry Series in 1992. She teaches at the University of Southern California.

KAREN BENKE's poetry and fiction have been published in several anthologies, including *An Intricate Weave: Women Write About Girls and Girlhood*. She has received grants from *Poets & Writers* and the Marin Arts Council, and teaches in the California Poets in the Schools program.

BRUCE BOND's third full-length book, *Radiography,* was released from BOA Editions last fall. His poems have recently appeared in *The Paris Review, The Ohio Review, The Yale Review, The Threepenny Review, Poetry,* and other journals. Currently he is Director of Creative Writing at the University of North Texas and Poetry Editor for *The American Literary Review.*

DAVID BOTTOMS is the author of two novels and four books of poems, most recently *Armored Hearts: Selected and New Poems.* Among the awards he has received for his work are the Walt Whitman Award, the Levinson Prize, an Ingram Merrill Award, and an Award in Literature from the American Academy and Institute of Arts and Letters.

JOEL BROUWER currently teaches creative writing at the University of Wisconsin–Madison. Other poems from his completed manuscript, *Exactly What Happened,* are forthcoming in *The Paris Review.* His chapbook of poems, *This Just In,* was published in March by the Beyond Baroque Literary Arts Center in Los Angeles.

PAM CROW is a clinical social worker. Her poems have appeared in *Calyx, Southern Poetry Review, The Seattle Review, Calapooya Collage,* and *The Florida Review,* among others. She lives in Portland, Oregon, with her partner of ten years and their two children, Zoe and Isaac.

MICHAEL CUDDIHY's *A Walled Garden* was published by Carnegie-Mellon in 1989. More recently, Rowan Tree Press issued his *Try Ironwood: An Editor Remembers,* with an introduction by Robert Hass. He is currently planning a polio memoir. Recent poems are in *Crazyhorse* and *Pequod.*

CHARD DENIORD is the author of *Asleep in the Fire* (Alabama, 1990). His poems have appeared recently in *The Pushcart Prize XXII, The Gettysburg Review, Ploughshares, The Iowa Review, Agni, The Harvard Review,* and *The Mississippi Review.* He teaches comparative religions, philosophy, and English at the Putney School in Vermont.

SHARON DOLIN is the author of *Heart Work* (Sheep Meadow, 1995) and *Climbing Mount Sinai,* a letterpress chapbook (Dim Gray Bar, 1996). Poems from a new manuscript are forthcoming in *The American Voice, The Amicus Journal, Boulevard, The Kenyon Review, Poetry International,* and *The Journal.* She teaches literature at Cooper Union and creative writing at The New School.

STEPHEN DUNN is the author of ten collections of poetry, most recently *Loosestrife* (Norton), which was a finalist for the National Book Critics Circle Award. Norton has just released his new book, *Riffs & Reciprocities: Prose Pairs.* He teaches at Richard Stockton College of New Jersey.

LAURA FARGAS's book, *An Animal of the Sixth Day,* was published by Texas Tech University Press in 1996. She lives in Washington, D.C., where she works as a lawyer litigating occupational safety and health cases for the government.

PATRICIA FARGNOLI is a clinical social worker from Keene, New Hampshire. She recently won the Robert Frost Literary Award from the Frost Foundation in Lawrence, Massachusetts. Her poems have been published or are forthcoming in *Poetry, Poetry Northwest, Indiana Review,* and *Prairie Schooner.* Just this spring, she was a resident of the MacDowell Colony.

HERMAN FONG's poems have appeared in *The Best American Poetry 1997, The Gettysburg Review, Indiana Review,* and elsewhere. Originally from Los Angeles, he is completing his M.F.A. in poetry at the University of Massachusetts at Amherst and divides his time between Southern California and Northampton, Massachusetts.

KENNY FRIES is the author of *Anesthesia: Poems* (Advocado) and *Body, Remember: A Memoir,* which was recently released in paperback by Plume. He is also the editor of *Staring Back: The Disability Experience from the Inside Out* (Plume). He received the Gregory Kolovakos Award for AIDS Writing for *The Healing Notebooks* and teaches in the M.F.A. in Writing program at Goddard College.

TED GENOWAYS's poetic sequence "The Bolt-Struck Oak" is from a book-length cycle; an earlier version was a finalist for last year's Yale Series of Younger Poets. Other poems have appeared in recent issues of *DoubleTake, New England Review,* and *Prairie Schooner.* He received this year's Guy Owen Poetry Prize from *Southern Poetry Review.*

DEBORA GREGER is the author of five books of poetry, most recently *Desert Fathers, Uranium Daughters* (Penguin, 1996). She teaches in the creative writing program at the University of Florida.

SAM HAMILL's poem in this issue is from *Gratitude,* which will be published by BOA Editions in August. His recent books include *The Essential Teachings of Chuang Tzu* and Kobayashi Issa's *The Spring of My Life* (both from Shambhala), and a second edition of his essays, *A Poet's Work* (Carnegie-Mellon).

JEFFREY HARRISON is the author of *The Singing Underneath* (Dutton, 1988), which was a National Poetry Series selection, and *Signs of Arrival* (Copper Beech, 1996). His poems have appeared in *The New Yorker, The New Republic, The Nation, The Paris Review, Poetry,* and other magazines. He is currently writer-in-residence at Phillips Academy in Andover, Massachusetts.

A. HEMON was born in Sarajevo, Bosnia-Herzegovina, where he lived until January 1992. His stories have been published in *TriQuarterly, Chicago Review,* and *Luisitania.* He won an Illinois Literary Award in 1997, and a collection of his stories, translated from English, has recently been published in Sarajevo. He lives in Chicago.

COLETTE INEZ is the author of eight books of poetry, most recently *Clemency* (Carnegie-Mellon, 1998). She has received fellowships from the Guggenheim and Rockefeller foundations, and twice from the NEA. She has taught poetry at Columbia University's writing program for more than a decade.

RUTH ELLEN KOCHER's poetry has recently appeared or is forthcoming in *Sojourner, The Missouri Review, African-American Review,* and *The Gettysburg Review.* She received her M.F.A. degree from Arizona State University and lives in Tempe, Arizona, where she is a doctoral student in American literature. Her poem in this issue comes from a manuscript-in-progress, *Desdemona's Fire.*

CHRISTINA LANZL has exhibited in galleries and museums in the U.S. and Germany. Her paintings and sculptures explore visual roots, and metaphorically address issues of identity and the nature of relationships. Her work is included in numerous private and corporate collections, and was recently featured on MTV's *Real World.* She lives in Boston and is also the executive director of the Brookline Arts Center.

DORIANNE LAUX is author of two collections of poetry from BOA Editions, *Awake* (1990) and *What We Carry* (1994), which was a finalist for the National Book Critics Circle Award. She co-authored *The Poet's Companion: A Guide to the Pleasures of Writing Poetry* with Kim Addonizio, and her recent poems have appeared in *The Kenyon Review, The American Poetry Review,* and elsewhere. She teaches at the University of Oregon.

WILLIAM LOGAN's most recent book of poems, *Vain Empires,* appeared from Penguin this spring. A book of early criticism, *All the Rage,* will be published shortly by the University of Michigan Press. He teaches at the University of Florida.

WILLIAM LYCHACK's fiction has appeared in *Quarterly West, The Sun, Witness,* and *The Best American Short Stories 1996.* He currently lives in New York City and is at work on a novel.

FRED MARCHANT is the author of *Tipping Point,* winner of the 1993 Washington Prize in poetry. He teaches in the English department at Suffolk University in Boston, where he also directs the creative writing program. He has recently completed his second book of poetry, *The Full Moon Boat.*

MORTON MARCUS's seventh book, *When People Could Fly,* a volume of prose poetry, was published by Hanging Loose Press in 1997. He has work in current issues of *The Prose Poem: An International Journal* and *The Barnabe Mt. Review,* as well as in the anthologies *The Party Train* and *American Poets Say Goodbye to the Twentieth Century.*

PETER MARCUS has had poems in *Poetry, New England Review, Shenandoah, Agni,* and in two previous issues of *Ploughshares.* His manuscript *Dark Remedies* has been a finalist or semifinalist for the Agnes Lynch Starrett, Brittingham, and Morse Prizes. He is a psychologist working at Western Connecticut State University's Counseling Center.

STEFANIE MARLIS makes her living as a freelance copywriter, producing everything from ads to catalogue copy. In this capacity, she has recently written a book entitled *The Art of the Bath* for Chronicle Books. New poems have appeared in *Arshile, The Gettysburg Review, Volt,* and *Zyzzyva.* This spring, Sarabande Books will publish her poetry collection, *rife.*

VALERIE MARTIN is the author of six books, including *Mary Reilly* and *The Great Divorce*. A novel, *Hell: An Italian Idyll*, and a biography, *Heaven: Scenes from the Life of St. Francis of Assisi*, are forthcoming from Doubleday later this year. She lives in upstate New York.

GWYN MCVAY is the author of two chapbooks of poems, *Brother Ikon* (Inkstone, 1995) and *This Natural History* (Pecan Grove, 1998). She is the editor of *So to Speak*, a feminist journal of language and art. Previously she worked with *The AWP Chronicle* and *The Journal of Buddhist Ethics*. Her work is forthcoming in *Calyx, Sulfur*, and *Poetry New York*.

JOSEPH MILLAR has just left his job as a telephone installation foreman to try his hand at teaching. In 1995 he won the Montalvo Biennial Poetry Competition, judged by Garrett Hongo, and placed second in the National Writers' Union Competition, judged by Philip Levine. He lives in Eugene, Oregon.

CAROL MUSKE's two most recent books are *An Octave Above Thunder: New and Selected Poems* (Penguin, Carnegie-Mellon) and *Women and Poetry: Truth, Autobiography, and the Shape of the Self*. The recipient of the Library of Congress's Witter-Bynner Fellowship for 1997–98, she teaches creative writing at the University of Southern California.

JOYCE CAROL OATES is the author, most recently, of the novel *My Heart Laid Bare* and *New Plays*. She teaches at Princeton University.

SUZANNE PAOLA has poems appearing in *The Partisan Review, Shenandoah*, and *The Notre Dame Review*, and essays in *American Literary Review* and *Boulevard*. Her third book of poems, *Bardo*, will appear in October from the University of Wisconsin Press as its Brittingham winner.

LINDA PASTAN's ninth book of poems, *An Early Afterlife*, has been issued in paperback by Norton. *Carnival Evening: New and Selected Poems: 1968–1998* is due out in April. She recently served as Poet Laureate of Maryland.

DONALD PLATT's first book of poetry, *Fresh Peaches, Fireworks, & Guns*, won the Verna Emery Prize and was published by Purdue University Press in 1994. He was awarded an NEA fellowship in 1996 and the Paumonak Poetry Prize in 1994. New work has appeared or is forthcoming in *The Southern Review, Western Humanities Review*, and *The Paris Review*. He teaches at the State University of West Georgia.

LIZ ROSENBERG's most recent book, a volume of prose poems, is due out in 1998 from The Mammoth Press. She has also written and edited several books for young readers, including *The Invisible Ladder*, winner of the 1997 Bank Street Claudia Lewis Poetry Award. She teaches English and creative writing at the State University of New York at Binghamton.

KAY RYAN has written four books of poetry, most recently *Elephant Rocks* (Grove, 1996). Her work is represented in *The Best of the Best American Poetry* (Scribner, 1998). She is the recipient of an Ingram Merrill Award and two Pushcart Prizes.

GERALD SHAPIRO's stories have appeared recently in *The Missouri Review, The Gettysburg Review, The Southern Review,* and *Witness.* His first collection of stories, *From Hunger,* was published by the University of Missouri Press in 1993. He received an NEA fellowship in 1995. He teaches fiction writing at the University of Nebraska–Lincoln.

PETER JAY SHIPPY has recently published poems in *Denver Quarterly* and plays in *Rosebud.* He is on the faculty of Emerson College.

KELLY SIMON's short fiction and travel stories have appeared in *The Quarterly* (volumes 20 and 21), *The Santa Clara Review, The Washington Post, Travelers' Tales: Hong Kong* and *Travelers' Tales: Food, Grand Tour,* and elsewhere. The vignettes in this issue are from a work-in-progress. She lives in San Francisco.

VIRGIL SUAREZ was born in Havana, Cuba, in 1962. He is the author of four novels, a story collection, and a collection of poetry and memoir, *Spared Angola: Memories from a Cuban-American Childhood.* He has also edited two bestselling anthologies with his wife, Delia Poey. More recently, he co-edited an anthology of Latino poetry, *Paper Dance,* with Victor Hernández Cruz and Leroy Quintana. He teaches at Florida State University in Tallahassee, where he lives with his family.

EVE SUTTON was the 1996 winner of the *The Writer Magazine*/Emily Dickinson Award from the Poetry Society of America. Her poetry has been pressed into bricks for a public art project, displayed in Congressional offices, and archived in the Department of Special Collections at Stanford University Libraries. She lives and teaches in Northern California.

DAVID WAGONER has published fifteen books of poems, most recently *Walt Whitman Bathing* (Illinois, 1996). His *Collected Poems* will appear next year. He edits *Poetry Northwest* for the University of Washington. He won the Lilly Prize in 1991.

DAVID FOSTER WALLACE's most recent books are *Infinite Jest,* a novel, and *A Supposedly Fun Thing I'll Never Do Again,* a collection of essays. He lives in Bloomington, Illinois.

RENÉE & THEODORE WEISS, editors of the *Quarterly Review of Literature* for over fifty years, have recently taken to writing poems together, and are putting the finishing touches to a volume. This past year PEN gave them a lifetime achievement award for editing. Theodore also received the 1997 Oscar Williams & Gene Derwood Award for his poetry.

ROBERT WRIGLEY's most recent book, *In the Bank of Beautiful Sins* (Penguin, 1995), won the San Francisco Poetry Center Book Award, and was a finalist for the Lenore Marshall Award. He lives with his family in the Clearwater River canyon in Idaho.

AL YOUNG is the author of *Conjugal Visits, Drowning in the Sea of Love, Heaven: Collected Poems,* and numerous other books of poetry, fiction, and nonfiction. Recently he edited *African American Literature: A Brief Introduction and Anthology.*

SUBSCRIBERS Please feel free to contact us via e-mail with address changes (the post office usually will not forward journals) or any problems with your subscription. Our e-mail address is: pshares@emerson.edu. Also, please note that on occasion we exchange mailing lists with other literary magazines and organizations. If you would like your name excluded from these exchanges, simply send us an e-mail message or a letter stating so.

~

SUBMISSION POLICIES *Ploughshares* is published three times a year: usually mixed issues of poetry and fiction in the Spring and Winter and a fiction issue in the Fall, with each guest-edited by a different writer. We welcome unsolicited manuscripts from August 1 to March 31 (postmark dates). All submissions sent from April to July are returned unread. In the past, guest editors often announced specific themes for issues, but we have revised our editorial policies and no longer restrict submissions to thematic topics. Submit your work at any time during our reading period; if a manuscript is not timely for one issue, it will be considered for another. Send one prose piece and/or one to three poems at a time (mail genres separately). Poems should be individually typed either single- or double-spaced on one side of the page. Prose should be typed double-spaced on one side and be no longer than twenty-five pages. Although we look primarily for short stories, we occasionally publish personal essays/memoirs. Novel excerpts are acceptable if self-contained. Unsolicited book reviews and criticism are not considered. Please do not send multiple submissions of the same genre, and do not send another manuscript until you hear about the first. Additional submissions will be returned unread. No more than a total of three submissions per reading period, please. Mail your manuscript in a page-size manila envelope, your full name and address written on the outside, to the "Fiction Editor," "Poetry Editor," or "Nonfiction Editor." Unsolicited work sent directly to a guest editor's home or office will be ignored and discarded; guest editors are formally instructed not to read such work. All manuscripts and correspondence regarding submissions should be accompanied by a self-addressed, stamped envelope (S.A.S.E.) for a response. Expect three to five months for a decision. Do not query us until five months have passed, and if you do, please write to us, including an S.A.S.E. and indicating the postmark date of submission, instead of calling. Simultaneous submissions are amenable as long as they are indicated as such and we are notified immediately upon acceptance elsewhere. We cannot accommodate revisions, changes of return address, or forgotten S.A.S.E.'s after the fact. We do not reprint previously published work. Translations are welcome if permission has been granted. We cannot be responsible for delay, loss, or damage. Payment is upon publication: $25/printed page, $50 minimum per title, $250 maximum per author, with two copies of the issue and a one-year subscription.

Say That! Productions

presents

≈ *ONE SIDE OF THE RIVER* ≈

36 poets of Cambridge and Somerville read their work as part of the 70th Anniversary celebration for The Grolier Poetry Book Shop

Charles Coe in the studio

Photo: copyright © 1998, Emily Hiestand

Jonathan Aaron ✦ Pam Alexander ✦ David Barber
Frank Bidart ✦ Laure-Anne Bosselaar ✦ Lucie Brock-Broido
Kurt Brown ✦ Gail Burton ✦ Mary Campbell ✦ Charles Coe
Andrea Cohen ✦ Henri Cole ✦ Martha Collins
Steven Cramer ✦ Susan Donnelly ✦ David Ferry
Kinereth Gensler ✦ Miriam Goodman ✦ Stratis Haviaras
Craig Hickman ✦ Emily Hiestand ✦ Marie Howe
Diana der-Hovanessian ✦ Teresa Iverson ✦ Gail Mazur
Robert Pinsky ✦ Liam Rector ✦ David Rivard ✦ Katrina Roberts
Peter Sacks ✦ Catherine Sasanov ✦ Lloyd Schwartz
Tom Sleigh ✦ Sue Standing ✦ Stephen Tapscott ✦ Mark Wagner

Set of two CDs, beautifully recorded and designed, for $29.95 at:

Harvard Square: The Grolier Poetry Book Shop,
Wordsworth Books, Harvard Bookstore, Harvard Coop

Concord: The Concord Bookshop

Boston: Waterstone's Booksellers

BENNINGTON WRITING SEMINARS

MFA *in Writing and Literature*
Two-Year Low-Residency Program

A. BLAKE GARDNER

FICTION
NONFICTION
POETRY

Jane Kenyon Poetry Scholarships available
For more information contact:
Writing Seminars
Box PL
Bennington College
Bennington, VT 05201
802-440-4452, Fax 802-447-4269

Miami University Press
OXFORD, OHIO

Poetry Series

For individuals call Pathway Book Service
(800) 345-6665 or
For trade call Ingram Book Company
(800) 937-8200
or Baker & Taylor (800) 775-1100

BRILLIANT WINDOWS
Larry Kramer

92 pp.
$19.95 cloth ISBN 1-881163-22-9
$11.95 paper ISBN 1-881163-23-7

I've been a fervent admirer of Larry Kramer's poems for years, as his is. . .a rare poetic intelligence whose surfaces and depth continually surprise and delight his readers. This is a remarkable and moving book.
—Lynne McMahon

Lyrically charged, passionately conceived, completely free of the moribund trappings of literary fashion, the music of these poems rises to the pitch of their grandly secular vision. —Sherod Santos

KISSES
Steve Orlen

73 pp.
$19.95 cloth ISBN 1-881163-20-2
$11.95 paper ISBN 1-881163-21-0

Orlen is a wonderful poet and one of the best practitioners of free verse writing today. The sounds of his poems bang and glide. Most fine poetry strikes the mind and heart. This is true of Orlen as well, but his poems also strike the ear. They feel good in the mouth. —Stephen Dobyns

Orlen's Bridge of Sighs, like Eliot's "Prufrock," is filled with many human voices, but they are the voices around us, the recognizable voices of people we know too well. . . . He builds from memory, from old photographs, mental snapshots of the past, and he knows where to break a line and also how to break your heart.
—Mark Hillringhouse in *The Literary Review*

WHAT WIND WILL DO
Debra Bruce

59 pp.
$19.95 cloth ISBN 1-881163-18-0
$11.95 paper ISBN 1-881163-19-9

I admire Debra Bruce's adroit use of form. Through it, paradoxically, she has acquired the freedom to confront subjects that range from cancer to infertility and she does so with grace. —Maxine Kumin

Along with such poets as Marilyn Hacker, Jane Kenyon, and Mary Oliver, Bruce has given us another woman's voice we have to listen to!
—Julia Alvarez

Announcing Boston Review's first annual

P•ETRY CONTEST

Judged by Jane Miller

$1,000 First Prize

Deadline: June 15, 1998

Complete guidelines: The winning poet will receive $1,000 and have his or her work published in the October/November 1998 issue of *Boston Review*. Submit up to five unpublished poems, no more than 10 pages total. A $10 entry fee, payable to *Boston Review* in the form of a check or money order, must accompany all submissions. Entries must be postmarked no later than June 15, 1998. Simultaneous submissions are allowed if the *Review* is notified of acceptance elsewhere. Manuscripts must be submitted in duplicate, with a cover note listing the author's name, address, and phone number; names should not be on the poems themselves. Manuscripts will not be returned; enclose a SASE for notification of winner. All entrants will receive a one-year subscription to the *Review* beginning with the October/November 1998 issue. Send all submissions to: Poetry Contest, *Boston Review*, E53-407, MIT, Cambridge MA 02139; (617) 494-0708.

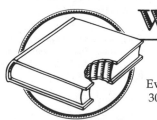

Be an Expatriate Writer

Ninth Annual
Ploughshares International Writing Seminar
Kasteel Well, The Netherlands

June 29 - July 8, 1998

"Definitely the most detailed, attentive response I've received in my writing life."

Join a diverse, intimate community of selected writers for an intensive, team-taught fiction seminar or memoir workshop.

Work closely with a distinguished faculty on strategies for revision. Develop your ideas in designated writing time. Return home with an improved draft and redefined objectives.

Be motivated by the opportunity to write – and re-write – in the tranquillity of a Dutch Renaissance castle.

The Faculty

FICTION:
Alexandra Marshall, author of a nonfiction book and four novels, including *Gus in Bronze* and, most recently, *Something Borrowed.*

Pamela Painter, author of the story collection *Getting To Know The Weather,* and co-author of *What If? Exercises for Fiction Writers.*

Thomas E. Kennedy, author of three novels and two story collections, including *The Book of Angels* and *Drive, Dive, Dance, and Fight,* as well as four volumes of literary criticism.

Askold Melnychuk, author of *What is Told?,* a New York Times Notable Book of 1995, Editor of *Agni,* and current recipient of a Writer's Award from the Lila Wallace Reader's Digest Fund.

MEMOIR:
Alexandra Johnson, nationally published writer and author of *The Hidden Writer,* winner of the PEN/Jerard Fund Award, teaches Memoir at Wellesley and Harvard Extension.

Visiting Writer

James Carroll, author of *The City Below* and eight previous novels, Boston Globe regular columnist, and winner of the 1996 National Book Award for his memoir, *An American Requiem.*

"Because of its non-hierarchical nature, its limited number of participants, and the mix of writing time with workshop time and other events, this is the best seminar I've ever attended."

The seminar is sponsored and administered by Emerson College and inspired by the literary traditions of the journal *Ploughshares,* an Emerson College publication. Four academic credits are offered. All manuscripts submitted with applications and received by April 1 are considered for the $1,000 Robie Macauley Fellowship.

For a brochure and application to the seminar, contact:

David Griffin, Assistant Director of Continuing Education,
Emerson College, 100 Beacon Street, Boston, MA 02116 USA
Tel: 617-824-8567, Fax: 617-824-8618, E-Mail: dgriffin@emerson.edu